CULTURAL GEMS:
An Eclectic Look
At Unique
United States Libraries

CULTURAL GEMS:
An Eclectic Look
At Unique
United States Libraries

Mary Buckingham Maturi

Mary Buckingham Maturi

Richard J. Maturi

Richard J. Maturi

21ST CENTURY PUBLISHERS

Library of Congress Catalog Card Number: 95-090555

Maturi, Mary Buckingham & Richard J.
    Cultural Gems: An Eclectic Look at Unique United
    States Libraries / Mary Buckingham Maturi and
    Richard J. Maturi
            p. cm.
Includes Index.
ISBN 0-9607298-1-X
1. Public libraries (U.S.)—Guidebooks. 2. Architecture. 3. History. 4. Popular culture. I. Maturi, Mary Buckingham & Richard J. II. Title: Cultural Gems: An Eclectic Look at Unique United States Libraries.

1 2 3 4 5 6 7 8 9 0

21st Century Publishers
1320 Curt Gowdy Drive
Cheyenne, Wyoming 82009

This book is dedicated to librarians throughout the nation who have instilled in children a desire to read everything from the adventures of "Chatterbox the Red Squirrel" to the "Hardy Boys" and "Nancy Drew" to the classics.

We extend our thanks to the State Librarians and State Historical Officers who recommended libraries for inclusion in this book. We thank the participating libraries for their work in providing history and photographs to make this collection of libraries possible. Special thanks to Garth Oldham for his endless hours of design and layout expertise.

We also wish to thank Dr. DeVon Carlson, Dean Emeritus of the School of Architecture and Planning at the University of Colorado in Boulder and Dr. James O. Rose, Director/Architectural Engineering at the University of Wyoming in Laramie for their expertise in helping us to recognize major architectural styles. It should be noted that many American library buildings consist of a combination of architectural elements borrowed from several styles.

Finally, thanks to Jane Pilley, Bertha, Muriel and Richard for their assistance in editing this book and to photographer Laurie Warner for her help in selecting the library pictures.

Front and back cover Photos: Courtesy of The Brumback
                                 Library, Van Wert, Ohio

Design by Seraph Print & Design, Cheyenne, Wyoming

Table of Contents

Preface

Our love of libraries was rekindled during our 1993 "Wyoming to Wall Street" trip along the Lincoln Highway route in our 1936 Oldsmobile. During that journey, we encountered many interesting libraries encompassing a variety of architectural styles. But even more important, no matter what time of day we stopped at the libraries across the nation, they were filled with people of all ages. Without a doubt, today's libraries have truly become the nation's cultural centers.

We invite you to join us on a voyage through "Cultural Gems: An Eclectic Look at Unique United States Libraries." The following pages are filled with a broad panorama of interesting histories and photographs of the civic buildings bringing culture and knowledge to the citizens of metropolitan cities, small towns and farm communities from coast-to-coast.

"Cultural Gems" is a unique reference geared to pique the interest of every lover and student of libraries, popular culture, architecture and history. Black and white photographs and illustrations accent the architectural detail covering a wide spectrum of styles from Classical Revival to Prairie to Pueblo.

Contrast the grandeur of the Folger Shakespeare Library in the District of Columbia with the distinctive stone structure of the Samuel H. Wentworth Library in Center Sandwich, New Hampshire. Discover the unexpected beauty of libraries in "off the beaten path" destinations like The Brumback Library in Van Wert, Ohio and the Ponca City Library in Ponca City, Oklahoma.

Sit back and enjoy a tour of the rich diversity of America's libraries.

Mary Buckingham Maturi
Richard J. Maturi
Cheramie, Wyoming

Special Note to Librarians: If you would like your library to be considered for "More Cultural Gems," please send a brief 3-4 typed page history (including dedication date, architect, architectural style and unique attributes) and good quality photograph of your library to 21st Century Publishers, 1320 Curt Gowdy Drive, Cheyenne, Wyoming 82009.

Other Books By Richard J. Maturi
—Wall Street Words   —Main Street Beats Wall Street
—Stock Picking   —The Hometown Investor
—Divining the Dow   —Money Making Investments
—The 105 Best Investments for the 21st Century

Also by Mary Buckingham Maturi and Richard J. Maturi
—Wyoming: Off the Beaten Path

I. Libraries in America

Church/University/Subscription Libraries

The establishment of libraries in America predates the Revolution. To be sure, private book collections existed from the earliest days of the colonies in the New World. Among the first libraries available to the common man were those established by Anglican clergyman, Thomas Bray. He developed a number of eastern seaboard parish libraries during his tenure as commissary to Maryland in the early eighteenth century.

Outside of the church influence, the first library in America was founded in 1638 at Harvard University. In later years, "social libraries" sprouted up, providing access to a circulating collection of materials and, in many cases, a reading room. Access to the social libraries' resources was typically by subscription, a fee paid to become a partnership owner or stockholder in the library. It thus limited library access only to the country's most influential and prosperous citizens. Benjamin Franklin and several friends established "The mother of all North American subscription libraries," The Philadelphia Library Company in 1731.

An offshoot of the social library, the Boston Athenaeum founded in 1807, catered to that city's most prominent citizens. Similar athenaeums sprung up in other major cultural centers of the period such as New York, Providence and Salem.

Free Libraries

Peterboro, New Hampshire claims the distinction of the first public library in America and the oldest free public library in the world supported by taxation. In the nineteenth century many social libraries were converted to public libraries open equally to all citizens.

By 1876 there were nearly 3,700 libraries of all types in the United States compared to less than 800 only a quarter of a century earlier. The centennial year proved to be another important event in the history of American libraries with the founding of the American Library Association (ALA) at a Philadelphia meeting of the country's librarians.

The driving force behind the ALA was Melvil Dewey, who also launched the "Library Journal" and instituted the Dewey Decimal Classification System that same year. Prior to Dewey's innovation, librarians numbered books consecutively as they acquired them and filed them on shelves without any regard to subject matter.

The Library of Congress

President John Adams approved legislation for the founding of the Library of Congress and appropriation of $5,000 to purchase books "for the use of Congress" after it moved from Philadelphia to the new capital city of Washington, in the District of Columbia, in 1800. Book lover, President Thomas Jefferson, approved legislation in 1802 that created the appointment of the Librarian of Congress by the President and granted Congress the power to establish Library of Congress operating rules and regulations.

As its name implies, the main mission of the Library of Congress was to serve the research needs of Congress. However, it was also open to the general public. The present Library of Congress facility opened in 1897 and has had several additions.

The Carnegie Legacy

The Andrew Carnegie legacy in the establishment of numerous public libraries across the nation is well known. Carnegie granted construction funds for 1,679 public libraries in 1,412 communities across the country, many of which had no public library prior to their Carnegie Library. Perhaps less understood is the fact that of the more than 2,500 Carnegie Libraries less than a third actually bore the Carnegie name and 33 percent were built outside of the United States in other English speaking countries such as Australia, Canada, Great Britain, New Zealand, Scotland, South Africa and the West Indies.

In fact, Mr. Carnegie's first philanthropic library gift was to his hometown of Dunfermline, Scotland in 1881. Carnegie also financed the construction of 108 libraries on college campuses and endowments to such universities as the University of Chicago, University of Denver, University of Michigan and University of North Carolina.

During the first 29 years, library design was left up to the officials where the library was to be located. At the urging of Mr. Carnegie's secretary, James Bertram, Carnegie instituted an architectural review of each proposed library beginning in 1910 in order to prevent waste and misuse of funds for nonfunctional features.

Another requirement for receiving a Carnegie library grant that proved too prohibitive for a number of communities applying for funding was the annual maintenance agreement requiring the communities to pledge 10 percent (with a minimum of $1,000) of the Carnegie grant amount for annual maintenance of the library facility. Some libraries receiving Carnegie grants had trouble satisfying the annual maintenance requirement. For example, Clarksville, Texas, which had received a $10,000 Carnegie Grant, defaulted on its annual maintenance pledge, shutting the library down after the first year due to lack of funds.

The advent of World War I and the accompanying shortage of manpower and materials put the grant program on hold. After the war, prior building commitments were honored but a Carnegie Corporation appraisal found many of the libraries providing poor service due to the lack of properly trained library personnel.

As a result, from 1926 until 1941 the Carnegie Corporation devoted a majority of its funds earmarked for libraries on grants for library training programs and endowments for the American Library Association, which it considered vital to the strengthening of the library profession. In 1925 Carnegie's contribution provided for the creation of the first graduate library school in the country at the University of Chicago. The first school of library science was established at Columbia University by Melvil Dewey in the 1880s.

Although Carnegie's formal schooling ended when he was only 12 years old, his access to the private library of Colonel James Anderson taught him the value of access to knowledge. As Carnegie recounted in his autobiography, "It was from my own early experience that I decided that there was no use to which money could be applied so productive of good to boys and girls who have good within them and ability and ambition to develop, as the founding of a public library in a community which is willing to support it as a municipal institution."

Overall, Carnegie contributed $56 million to library construction and over $33 million to improve library service between 1911 and 1961. Carnegie Libraries were constructed in 47 states and the District of Columbia; only Alaska, Delaware and Rhode Island were without a Carnegie Library.

In 1985 the Cooper-Hewitt Museum in New York City presented an exhibit of Carnegie Libraries, its program remarked on the architecture of Carnegie Libraries, "It's difficult to characterize the Carnegie Libraries as a group. The program was so vast and the circumstances for which these buildings were designed were so varied that perhaps it can only be said that in the aggregate they reflect the extraordinary richness of American architecture at the turn of the century."

The exhibit illustrated not only the geographic scope of Carnegie Libraries but also the skilled and diverse solutions developed by architects in response to designing a relatively new building type.

Carnegie library grants for buildings in the United States ranged from as little as $2,000 for the community of Raymond, New Hampshire (Dudley-Tucker Library) in 1906 to the $481,012 spent on the Carnegie Library in Alleghany, Pennsylvania in 1886. New York City came away with 66 Carnegie Libraries costing $5.2 million combined and Pittsburgh's nine Carnegie Libraries cost $1.16 million.

New York State garnered the greatest total amount of Carnegie funds for library buildings with $6,449,200 while Carnegie's home state of Pennsylvania captured $4,621,148, followed by Ohio with $2,871,483 and California with $2,776,987.

Wyoming ranked first in terms of the amount of Carnegie dollars appropriated per population with $114.20 per 100 population while Virginia came in last with $3.20 per 100 population. Four states ended up with Carnegie Libraries in nearly 100 or more communities: Indiana (155), California (121), Illinois (105), and Iowa (99).

In addition to the Carnegie Libraries which were built, another 225 proposed Carnegie Libraries never materialized for a variety of reasons including inability to financially support the 10 percent maintenance requirement, architectural disagreements, defeat by electorate, site problems, World War I, rising building costs, request for more funds, and donations by local philanthropists.

Local Benefactors

Carnegie was not alone in his desire to educate the populace and leave a lasting legacy. Many local philanthropists across the nation donated land and/or funds to construct local public libraries. In many cases the libraries bear the name of the benefactor or benefactors while in other cases the gifts were bequeathed anonymously. You will meet many of these philanthropists in the pages ahead.

Final Note

In this book we have concentrated for the most part on older libraries with a sprinkling of newer libraries to show some contemporary library architecture. As a result, there are a number of Carnegie Libraries represented in the following pages due to the impact Carnegie had on the library movement of that time period. However, we believe we have achieved a balance of Carnegie, other benefactors and local government funded libraries.

We concentrated more on older libraries because they are the ones most in danger of being destroyed due to expansion requirements, changing metropolitan patterns and urban renewal. We wanted to capture these cultural gems before they are lost forever.

II. Gulf and Eastern — Region

Bixby Memorial Free Library

258 Main Street
Vergennes, Vermont
05491

Dedication: 1912

Architecture: Classical
Revival

Photo courtesy of Bixby Memorial Free Library

Bixby Memorial Free Library
Vergennes, Vermont

William Gove Bixby, benefactor of the Bixby Memorial Free Library, engaged in a variety of business endeavors ranging from a Vergennes hardware store owned in conjunction with his father to banking, sheep ranching and operating grain elevators in Colorado. However, the bulk of his estate derived from his sister, Eleanor, who had been widowed by a wealthy Chicago hotel owner.

Mr. Bixby died in 1907, leaving the majority of his estate to establish a free public library in Vergennes. The cornerstone was laid in September 1911 and the library opened to the public in November 1912. Architect Frederick Frost of the New York firm of Trowbridge and Livingston employed Indiana limestone, Ionic columns, a large rotunda and yellow tapestry brick to create an impressive structure for Vergennes' less than 2,600 citizens.

The back of the library was curved to take advantage of the view. An interesting crosshatched window sits over the double oak doors of the main entrance. A white marble sculpture, "The Young Trumpeter," by noted sculptor Margaret Foley (who spent her childhood in Vergennes) graces the library interior, situated beneath a great stained glass dome. In 1936 summer resident Josephine Meneely donated collections of cup plates and paper weights to the library. Other interesting displays include paintings, models of historic ships and rotating exhibits of timely historic material.

A library collection of native Indian artifacts makes up one of the best selections of Indian material in Vermont. Likewise, the Vermont Room houses an extensive collection of Vermontiana.

James Blackstone Memorial Library

Branford, Connecticut

The James Blackstone Memorial Library began with a special charter from the Connecticut Legislature and approval by the Governor. The legislation vested control of the proposed library in a self-perpetuating Board of Trustees consisting of six Branford residents and the Yale University librarian.

Benefactor Timothy Beach Blackstone spent a life-long career with railroads, ending his career as President of the Chicago & Alton Railroad. In addition to providing the funds for the construction of the $300,000 James Blackstone Memorial Library (dedicated to his father), Timothy Blackstone also endowed the library with over $200,000 to ensure its operation and contributed 5,000 volumes toward the library's initial book acquisition program. Blackstone made his donation in 1893 and the library was dedicated on June 17, 1896.

Blackstone commissioned Chicago architect Solon S. Beman (architect for a number of Chicago World's Fair buildings) to design the Greek Revival structure. Beman patterned the library after the beautiful Erechtheum of the Athenian Acropolis using Ionic columns, a rotunda, a free standing marble staircase, and egg and dart molding to distinguish the memorial library.

The Latin cross layout is crafted out of light-tone Tennessee marble. Entrance to the library is gained through two highly ornamented bronze doors, weighing 2,000 pounds each. Solid oak wainscoting, polished marble piers and arches and mosaic marble floors add to the richness of the design. Beman contracted Oliver Dennet Grover of Chicago to prepare eight large dome murals illustrating the evolution of book making as well as eight medallion portraits of literary notables such as Hawthorne and Longfellow.

Photo courtesy of John Rowland Elliott

James Blackstone Memorial Library

758 Main Street
Branford, Connecticut
06405

Dedication: 1896

Architecture: Greek Revival

Bridgeville Public Library

Bridgeville, Delaware

The Bridgeville Public Library building originated in 1866 as the First Presbyterian Church of Bridgeville and served local inhabitants for nearly fifty years. During World War I the structure was put to use as both a school and a Red Cross Station. In 1917 the Tuesday Night Club (organized in 1896) purchased the building for $500 and later established a circulating library.

The last surviving president of the Tuesday Night Club, Mrs. Margaret R. Cannon (librarian for 33 years), and Mrs. Olivia Willin signed over the building in 1964 to the Bridgeville Public Library, Inc., which operates the library under contract with the Sussex County Department of Libraries and the Delaware State Division of Libraries.

The three-bay, one and one-half story frame, gable roofed building employs a center entrance through the base of the two-story bell tower (added around the turn of the century). A one-story wing (added in the 1890s) housed the main library for many years. A renovation of the main church room in 1965 provided more room for the library and special events. Major restoration work took place in 1990 in order to repair extensive damage caused by termites. The Bridgeville Public Library joined the ranks of the National Register of Historic Places in 1990.

Photo courtesy of Robert J. Bennett, CPP

Bridgeville Public Library

210 Market Street
Bridgeville, Delaware
19933

Dedication: 1866 as
First Presbyterian
Church of Bridgeville

Rededication: 1917 as
Tuesday Night Club
(literary society)

Rededication: 1964 as
Bridgeville Public
Library

Architecture: Gothic
Revival

Brown Public Library
Northfield, Vermont

The first circulating library in Northfield, Vermont traces back to 1825 and in 1856 the Vermont and Canada Railroad Association established a small library "for mental improvement" in the passenger depot. Seventy-five stockholders formed the Northfield Library Association in 1871, assessing members 50 cents annual dues and charging a 2 cent check out fee to members with 10 cents to non-shareholders.

In 1894 the Vermont Legislature passed an act authorizing the establishment of free public libraries. Northfield took advantage of this legislation and voted $50 for their library. The first free public library originated in 1896, located in the Paine Block. The Northfield Library Association donated its collection to the fledgling library. Proceeds from Northfield's dog tax were earmarked for the library beginning in 1897. Fires forced the library from the Paine Block and later from the Union Block in 1904 after which it was relocated to the house of E.K. Jones on South Main Street.

A former resident and official with the United Shoe Machinery Company in Boston, Mr. George Washington Brown, donated construction funds in excess of $20,000 for the Brown Public Library, in memory of his family. All the businesses in the town closed for the August 21, 1906, dedication ceremonies at the Methodist Church. The brick library featured granite trimmings, Ionic columns, intricately designed windows and an interior finished in cypress.

Strong community support is evidenced by the combined two hundred hours of service donated each month by over thirty volunteers. Although the library is funded by tax monies, the 175 members of the Friends of the Library raise money for special projects.

Photo courtesy of Brown Public Library

Brown Public Library

**South Main Street
Northfield, Vermont
05663**

Dedication: 1906

**Architecture: Classical
Revival**

Carnegie Branch Library

Chatham-Effingham-
Liberty Regional
Library

537 East Henry Street
Savannah, Georgia
31401

Dedication: 1914

Architecture: Prairie

Photo courtesy of Steve Bisson

Carnegie Branch Library

Savannah, Georgia

The historically significant Carnegie Branch Library in Savannah, Georgia represents the only example of Prairie style architecture in this Southern city. A committee of African-American citizens realized the need for a library in the black community and organized materials and fund raising with the help of area churches, civic organizations and residents.

In 1906 their efforts culminated in the opening of the Library for Colored Citizens of Savannah in a rented building on the northeast corner of Price and Hartridge Streets. As the library grew and needs increased, it obtained financial support from the City of Savannah and a Board of Curators was established.

The Board solicited and received $12,000 from the Carnegie Corporation for construction of a library building. That success prompted the raising of an additional $3,000 from local supporters for the acquisition of land on East Henry Street for the library.

The stately, two-story, red brick building was designed by Savannah architect Julian deBruyn Kops and constructed by William J. Ayers in 1914. The Board renamed the library, Carnegie Branch Library, in deference to Mr. Carnegie's generosity. In 1963 the library became part of the Savannah Public Library System, now the Chatham-Effingham-Liberty Regional Library.

Eufaula Carnegie Library

Eufaula, Alabama

At a special February 1903 meeting, the Eufaula City Council approved the appropriation of $1,000 annually to maintain the proposed library to be built with a $10,000 Carnegie Grant. The Council also appointed a Library Commission with the purpose of soliciting subscriptions and selecting a suitable library site.

Local architect, Charles A. Stephens, designed a two-story red brick structure with pressed yellow brick trim. Contractors broke ground in October 1903 and the dedication took place in the Spring of 1904.

The rectangular building features a hipped roof with 6-to-8 foot overhanging eaves. The front terrace is adorned with wrought-iron railing and lampposts on either side of the landing steps. Double glass doors, highlighted by a transom of colored leaded glass, lead into a marble mosaic tile foyer. A recessed balcony on the second story is adorned with four square columns and a wraparound wooden balustrade.

The upper floor houses an auditorium with a performance stage and dressing rooms. A large window with double hung sash and a colored glass transom is located at the rear of the stage. The Eufaula Carnegie Library utilized the auditorium for traveling attractions, public and private school plays, dances and fund raising activities.

Renovations in 1986 and a new addition in 1990 architecturally compliment the original 1904 structure and provide greater efficiency and more capacity to better serve the Eufaula Carnegie Library's patrons. The Alabama Historical Association Director, Larry Oakes, described the new addition as, "one of the finest additions to a historical structure that I have seen anywhere."

The Alabama Preservation Alliance presented the Eufaula Carnegie Library with an Honor Award in 1990 for the preservation and conservation of historical resources.

Photo courtesy of Barbara L. Kunkel, Photography, Abbeville, Alabama

Eufaula Carnegie Library

217 North Eufaula
Avenue
Eufaula, Alabama
36027

Dedication: 1904

Architecture: Italianate

Field Memorial Library

Conway, Massachusetts

The Field Memorial Library is the only building of this stature in the tiny hill town of Conway, Massachusetts. The impressive library owes its existence to the founder of the great Chicago department store bearing his name, Marshall Field and Company. Field grew up on the family farm and attended school in nearby Pumpkin Hollow.

In 1899 Field visited Conway to choose the site for the library he would dedicate in honor of his mother and father, John and Fidelia Nash Field. Special invitations to the July 13, 1901, dedication gathered Conway residents, distant native sons and daughters and librarians from near and far. In addition to donating the funds for the library construction, Field also endowed the library with $52,000 for the operation of the building. There is no public funding or public control. The Board of Trustees appoint their own successors with the approval of the judge of the Probate Court.

The Boston architectural firm of Shepley Rutan and Coolidge (now Shepley Bulfinch Richardson and Abbott) designed the library employing classical styling with exterior Bedford limestone and trimmings of grey granite. Large Ionic columns flank the portal and a twenty-five foot diameter copper dome rises forty-one feet above the sill. The interior is of the finest oak and marble, both domestic and imported. The rotunda is surrounded by Ionic columns of Brescia Violet marble, resting on a floor of richly colored marble mosaic. The building and its equipment represent an expenditure in excess of $100,000.

Heavy construction materials were delivered to the village on the Conway Electric Street Railway. The loaded cars were then transferred onto tracks temporarily laid on the surface of Main Street and rolled by gravity to the building site and later drawn back by horses.

Of all of his philanthrophic endeavors, Field once commented that building the Field Memorial Library had given him the greatest pleasure.

Photo courtesy of Nancy L. Dole, West County News

Field Memorial Library

One Elm Street
Conway, Massachusetts
01341

Dedication: 1901

Architecture: Classical Revival

Folger
Shakespeare
Library

201 East Capitol
Street, S.E.
Washington, D.C. 20003

Dedication: 1932

Architecture: Beaux-Arts

Photo by permission of the Folger Shakespeare Library

Folger Shakespeare Library

Washington, D.C.

Dedicated on April 23, 1932, the Folger Shakespeare Library contains the library, an exhibition gallery and a theater for public and educational programs. Designed by Philadelphia architect Paul Philippe Cret (also the designer of another "Cultural Gems" featured library, The Indianapolis-Marion County Public Library) in the Beaux-Arts tradition, the building features nine high-relief panels crafted by sculptor John Gregory and illustrating scenes from the playwright's most noted plays, including "A Midsummer Night's Dream," "Romeo and Juliet," "The Merchant of Venice" and "Hamlet."

Founded by industrialist (President of the Standard Oil Company of New York) Henry Clay Folger and his wife Emily Jordan, The Folger Library serves as a research library, museum and cultural center dedicated to Shakespeare and the Renaissance. Located next to the Library of Congress on Capitol Hill, the library, with marble exterior embellished by metalwork grilles, contains plaster ceilings, richly paneled walls, stone and tile floors and windows of leaded and stained glass which evoke an Elizabethan great house. Bas-reliefs of Pegasus, the symbol of lyric poetry, flank the two main doors while the masks of Tragedy and Comedy crown the porticos.

The Folgers' original collection of Shakespeareana remains the largest and most complete in existence today. Over 1,000 advanced scholars conduct independent research at the Library each year and its exhibitions, theatre performances and other events attract in excess of 200,000 visitors annually. The Folger Shakespeare Library is a tax-exempt cultural institution governed by the Trustees of Amherst College. Revenues are derived from a combination of endowment income (54%), contributions and grants (27%) and earned income (19%).

Perhaps Dr. Lucius C. Clark, Chancellor of the American University in Washington, D.C. at the time of the Library's dedication captured it best, "The Folger Shakespeare Library is more than a dream in marble. It is more than an outward frame for sheltering most beautiful volumes. It is a habitation."

Eleanor K. Freed Montrose Library

Houston, Texas

The building housing the Eleanor K. Freed Montrose Library has undergone a number of trials and transformations over the years. William Ward Watkin designed this Italian Romanesque structure of sand-colored hand made brick in the early 1940s as the Central Church of Christ. Construction was delayed due to shortages of materials during World War II. A special dispensation from the War Production Board in Washington, D.C. permitted the release of enough steel to complete construction.

Developer John Hansen eventually acquired the church property and in 1986 donated the sanctuary and the land on which it sits to the City of Houston in order to create a branch of the Houston Public Library in the area.

Ray Bailey Architects, Inc. of Houston designed the library around three main building exterior assets: the campanile (bell tower), the tall windows and large stained glass window over the portal. Inside, the architect used the 24-foot vaulted ceiling to create a breathtaking cantilevered mezzanine. Natural light from the tall windows fills both levels of the library. The Romanesque campanile now houses a large staircase which connects the library's two levels. A field-stone-paved entrance adjacent to the tower, gives the campanile added emphasis as an integral part of the library. The resurrected building underwent one additional change. In 1995 its name changed to the Eleanor K. Freed Montrose Library in dedication to a loyal and generous library patron.

Photo courtesy of Ivett Garza

Eleanor K. Freed Montrose Library

4100 Montrose Boulevard
Houston, Texas 77006

Dedication: Early 1940s as Central Church of Christ

Rededication: 1988 as Houston Public Library Montrose Branch

Rededication: 1995 as Eleanor K. Freed Montrose Library

Architecture: Italian Romanesque

Gardiner Public Library

Gardiner, Maine

Dedicated in 1881, the Gardiner Public Library was established by the Gardiner Library Association, which owns the land and building. Preceding the Library Association, there had been a library collection in Gardiner since 1786 with the Last Will and Testament of Dr. Sylvester Gardiner bequeathing books for a Gardiner Library and naming the Episcopal minister librarian.

The structure was designed by architect and sculptor Henry Richards, a descendent of Gardiner's first family and founder of Maine's oldest boys' camp. His wife, Laura, was one of the founding directors of the Gardiner Library Association and her mother authored "The Battle Hymn of the Republic." For over 100 years, the Richards family served as officers and directors of the Gardiner Library Association.

Richards used brick and sandstone accented by Flemish style gables to create a structure portraying strength. The inscription over the peaked doorway, "Forthright and Stalwart," fits such an impressive building. Richards' English schooling, prior to earning a degree from Harvard University, clearly shows in the English Renaissance exterior. The use of multiple dormers and triple-hung sash met the requirement for a well-lighted public library. The red mortared building owns the distinction of being the second public library in Maine.

The library continues to grow with the community. The R.P. Hazzard Room was added in 1930 to accommodate a bigger children's library area. The Hazzard room contains a large granite fireplace adorned with a mantle adaptation of one crafted in Southwest Norfolk, England in 1583. In 1960, the J. Walter Robinson Reference Wing was added and the Hazzard family once again provided a gift for the addition of the Burress Moore, III, Children's Room in 1977. Private monies funded the Community Room in 1985. The library operates as a city department, with a Board of Trustees, appointed by the Mayor. Participating towns each appoint one trustee.

Photo courtesy of Robert Darby: Photography of Architecture, Auburn, Maine

Gardiner Public Library

152 Water Street
Gardiner, Maine 04345

Dedication: 1881

Architecture: English
Renaissance

Handley Regional Library
Winchester, Virginia

Handley Regional Library serves Frederick County and Clarke County in addition to the residents of Winchester, Virginia. In 1895 Judge John Handley, a native of Ireland and a resident of Scranton, Pennsylvania bequeathed in excess of $1 million to Winchester. Two hundred and fifty thousand dollars were to be invested in State of Virginia bonds and used to build and equip a library after the interest and principal had grown to $500,000. The balance was used to set up an endowment to maintain the library.

Handley's interest in Winchester began in 1869 after he accepted a friend's invitation to visit the community. Over the years he visited Winchester many times and requested that he be buried in Winchester's Mt. Hebron Cemetery.

Construction began in 1907 and the Handley Library was completed in 1912. However, the library did not open until August 21, 1913, since the intervening time was needed to acquire a collection of 2,300 books and catalogue them.

New York architects Stewart Barney and Henry Otis Chapman designed the impressive structure in the Beaux-Arts style, employing elaborate ornamentation. Large Corinthian columns and a massive portico exemplify grandeur.

The library's plan resembles a book with the rotunda signifying the spine and the two wings of the library as the open book pages. The rotunda's dome is copper covered on the exterior and highlighted with stained glass on its interior.

A wing addition completed in 1979 enhances the library's ability to serve its patrons. Russell Bailey of Bailey and Gardner in Orange, Virginia, acted as consultant to Smithey and Boynton, Architects and Engineers of Roanoke, which designed the modern wing to compliment the original architecture. The addition won a First Honor Award from the American Institute of Architects.

Also in 1979, the library changed its name to the Handley Regional Library to reflect its new status as a regional library. It is listed on the National Register of Historic Places.

Photo courtesy of Handley Regional Library

Handley Regional Library

100 West Piccadilly
Street
Winchester, Virginia
22601

Dedication: 1913

Architecture: Beaux-Arts

Johnstown Public Library

38 South Market Street
Johnstown, New York
12095

Dedication: 1902

Architecture: French
Renaissance

Photo courtesy of Johnstown Public Library

Johnstown Public Library

Johnstown, New York

Sir William Johnson, Mohawk Baronet and New York's connection with the Iroquis Nation, maintained a working library in his home and shared his reading materials with his fellow Johnstown citizens until his death in 1774. Johnson is also credited with building the first free public school in New York. In addition, the Court House he had built in 1772 is the oldest active court house in the United States.

In 1836 Joseph Cuyler allowed a portion of his North Perry Street office to be used as a library with Johnstown residents permitted to borrow books on Saturday afternoons. The Johnstown Academy Library opened its doors to the general public in 1872. In 1886 the "King's Daughters" auxiliary of the YMCA, in conjunction with the YMCA, opened a fee-based reading room in the old McFarlain Building. The books used there were from the old Cady Mansion (family of Elizabeth Cady Stanton, the mother of women's rights).

Andrew Carnegie pledged $20,000 for a library in 1901 and later upped the amount to $25,000 after the city had raised $6,000 towards the project. Architects Fuller and Pitcher of Albany, New York designed a two-story French Renaissance structure using buff-pressed Roman brick accented with terra cotta trimmings and quoins.

The contractor, Joseph Hess, erected two tall stone columns and two light standards on each side of the library's main entrance. The foundation consists of a combination of Warsaw bluestone and Indiana limestone. Eight pillars in the main entrance foyer support a dome eighteen feet in diameter. The interior oak woodwork exudes a warm, comfortable feeling as do three fireplaces located throughout the building.

During 1976-1977, a mezzanine was added along the full width of the two-story rear section of the library. The Johnstown Public Library is in the process of meeting the structural requirements of the Americans With Disabilities Act and considering expansion options, while maintaining the architectural integrity of this cultural gem.

B.F. Jones
Memorial Library

663 Franklin Avenue
Aliquippa, Pennsylvania
15001

Dedication: 1929

Architecture: Italian
Renaissance

Photo courtesy of Helen Scott

B.F. Jones Memorial Library

Aliquippa, Pennsylvania

The impressive B. F. Jones Memorial Library in Aliquippa (formerly Woodlawn), Pennsylvania derives from the generosity of Mrs. Elisabeth M. Horne, who funded the land purchase and construction costs of the library built in memory of her father, Benjamin Franklin Jones Sr., one of the founders of Jones & Laughlin (J & L) Steel Corporation.

Mrs. Horne engaged the Pittsburgh architectural firm of Bartholomew & Smith to design a "restrained" Italian Renaissance structure in downtown Aliquippa. The flat Indiana limestone facade is embellished with large columns supporting intricate scrollwork above the tall windows. The words: Philosophy, Biology, Astronomy, Fiction, History, Science, Painting, Music, Sculpture, Drama, Poetry and Romance are carved into the wall face below the roofline of an elaborate cast bronze cheneau. B.F. Jones Memorial Library is engraved above the bronze main entrance doors and flanked by ornamental fasces and draping.

Inside, a larger-than-lifesize statue of B.F. Jones greets visitors from a base of green Vermont marble. Above, a recreated ornate Italian ceiling completes the memorial foyer. Marble and decorative plaster medallions adorn the main reading room. Interior doors are crafted from solid mahogany and brass. Wrought iron screens separate the lobby from the reference and reading rooms. The library has continued to serve the changing educational and cultural needs of its patrons as envisioned by its benefactor Mrs. Horne.

Aliquippa's B.F. Jones Memorial Library is listed in the Pennsylvania Inventory of Historic Places and on the National Register of Historic Places.

Laughlin Memorial Library

Eleventh Street & Maplewood Avenue
Ambridge, Pennsylvania 15003

Dedication: 1929

Architecture: Italian Renaissance

Photo courtesy of Gilbert Photography

Laughlin Memorial Library
Ambridge, Pennsylvania

The Laughlin Memorial Library in Ambridge, Pennsylvania commemorates the memory of Alexander Laughlin, Jr. (1889-1926), a Major in the American Expeditionary Forces of the World War 1918-1919 and President of Central Tube Company.

Pittsburgh architect Colonel Eric Fisher Wood designed the Italian Renaissance building using Indiana limestone for the exterior surface. Roman Doric columns and arches guide the visitor from the exterior portico to the cast bronze entrance doors. The portico ceiling is overlaid with an Italian Renaissance design.

Inside, sixteen 13-foot-high monolithic columns of Italian Black and Gold marble form a central square. Quarried from the top of an Italian island mountain (600 feet above the Mediterranean Sea), these columns are said to be the largest monolithic columns of this type of marble in the world. The square is floored with English Vein Marble and lighted from above by clerestory windows. Genuine gold accents the architectural details of the library's circulation room.

A bronze tablet of Major Laughlin, executed by noted sculptor, Bryant Baker, covers the wall opposite the main library entrance. The tablet's figures of Industry and Patriotism illustrate Laughlin's ties to manufacturing life and his patriotic services during World War I. Decorative canvas or finely woven jute tapestry hang on the interior plaster walls. The Laughlin Memorial Library was dedicated on July 6, 1929.

Madison Public Library

Madison, Maine

Madison's Ladies Non-Sectarian Club (formed in 1855) petitioned a Justice of the Peace in 1886 to call a meeting for the purpose of incorporating a library association. With $500 in assets, the Madison Library Association opened its doors in a second floor room of the Towne Block. The library moved several times over the next two decades. In 1905 Carnegie pledged $8,000 for the construction of a free library and the town voted to raise the necessary ten percent annual building maintenance funds required by Carnegie.

The red brick hexagonal library features a pyramidal lantern high above the second floor balcony. Reading rooms flank both sides of the lobby. Two tall pillars at the top of wide granite steps guard the library's entrance and support the beam with LIBRARY carved into the stone. After the completion of the library in 1907, a Soldier's Monument was placed on the lawn to commemorate Madison's veterans of all wars.

During World War II a false ceiling was installed over the lobby. The space above the false ceiling is now used to store local historical artifacts. Money raised by the Madison Sorosis Club funded conversion of a basement area into a children's room in 1968. A $1,000 memorial gift trust fund begun in 1979 by the Madison's Woman's Club has grown considerably, enabling the Trustees to purchase additional books. A $75,000 renovation in 1984 provided handicapped access and converted space into more efficient usage. The Madison Public Library was granted placement on the National Register of Historic Places in 1989.

Photo courtesy of Shirley K. Richard

Madison Public Library

12 Old Point Avenue
Madison, Maine 04950

Dedication: 1907

Architecture: Eclectic

Manchester City Library

405 Pine Street
Manchester,
New Hampshire 03104

Dedication: 1914

Architecture: Italian
Renaissance

Photo courtesy of Bob La Pree, Contoocook, New Hampshire

Manchester City Library

Manchester, New Hampshire

Manchester's library roots reach back to September 6, 1854, when the city received the Manchester Athenaeum, a subscription library, by charter. Manchester businessman and philanthropist Frank Pierce Carpenter donated the present library as a memorial to his wife, Elenora Blood Carpenter. Manchester hired a team of architects, Edward L. Tilton of New York and Edgar A.P. Newcomb of Honolulu to design an Italian Renaissance style Carpenter Memorial Library opposite Manchester's Victory Park. Tilton and Newcomb also used elements of Beaux-Arts architectural styling. The library dedication took place on November 18, 1914.

The Concord granite base and steps lead up to an impressive two-story structure faced with white marble and roofed with grey green Spanish tile. Two bronze light standards guide patrons to the main entrance featuring massive doors and grillework weighing two and a half tons. Above the grillework, a marble keyblock in the shape of an owl symbolizes Learning. Other carved ornamentation and their symbolism include torches for Light, circles for Infinity, lintels for Repose, panels for Rectitude, arches for Assiduity and Persistence and the fret or waves beating against the doors of Knowledge. Tall, arched windows provide ample natural light to the main floor.

Inside, the richly ornamented dome rises forty feet above the floor while Botticino marble wainscots the area and eight columns of rich Lastavena marble reach skyward.

The Manchester City Library has provided a rich legacy to the city but it is nearing capacity after over eighty years of service.

Mauney Memorial Library

100 South Piedmont
Avenue
Kings Mountain,
North Carolina 28086

Dedication: early 1920s
as Dr. J.G. Hord
Mansion

Rededication: 1947 as
Mauney Memorial
Library

Architecture: Roman
Classicism

Photo courtesy of Ronnie Hawkins

Mauney Memorial Library
Kings Mountain, North Carolina

The first Kings Mountain library began as a collection of donated books located in a room above Keeter's Department Store. It moved several times, residing in the old Town Hall on Cherokee Street and later in two basement rooms of the new City Hall on North Piedmont. The Mauney Memorial Library came into existence in 1947 when the children of Jacob S. and Margaret Julietta Rudisill Mauney purchased the Hord mansion and donated it for the express purpose of a library for the citizens of Kings Mountain. Mr. and Mrs. J.S. Mauney were among the founders of Kings Mountain and established the first cotton mill in the town.

The two-story Hord Roman Classicism mansion was constructed in the early 1920s using yellow brick. Four massive Doric columns span the entrance steps and support the front porch and the tile room. Keystone arches over the windows add architectural detail and strength. The front door is embellished with beveled leaded glass and wide decorative molding.

The interior features a beautiful oak stairway and intricate wainscoting adorns the entryway and stairwell. A major 1988 renovation, designed by architect Roger Holland, added a 150-seat auditorium, an enlarged nonfiction room and a new Carolina room while preserving the character of the original building.

Over the years, the Mauney Library shared the former mansion with a teacherage, a type of boarding house for out-of-town single teachers. Income from the teacherage continued until 1972. In 1976 two junior rooms were dedicated to the memory of the librarian's daughter, Jan Marion Fryer, who had conducted story hours in the summers. The Carolina Room houses historical materials and is dedicated to Bonnie Mauney Summers, who researched and wrote about the history of Kings Mountain.

The Mauney Memorial Library is a municipal library funded by the city, county and state.

Mirror Lake Carnegie Library

St. Petersburg, Florida

One could not ask for a better location. The Mirror Lake Carnegie Library overlooks Mirror Lake and affords patrons a view of Tampa Bay only five blocks away. It is also located in the heart of St. Petersburg's beautiful historic downtown district.

A Carnegie Grant in the amount of $17,500 provided the funds for the first permanent home for the St. Petersburg Library. Henry Whitfield, a noted New York architect associated with the Carnegie Foundation (also a brother of Mrs. Carnegie), designed the building in the Beaux-Arts style with classical detailing befitting the area. The cornerstone was laid on December 19, 1914, and the library was opened to the public on December 1, 1915.

The buff colored brick is accented with decorative cast concrete ornamentation. Plain pilasters break the facade into five bays and frame the windows. The large cornice features dental molding and a large shell design over the entrance. Clay barrel tiles cap the structure.

In 1965 a larger Main Library opened, making the Mirror Lake Carnegie Library a branch. The building underwent a complete exterior restoration in 1990 under the guidance of the architectural firm of Willingham & Associates. Oakhurst Construction Company completed interior restoration in late 1993 and a new $1 million addition designed by Harvard, Jolly, Clees and Toppe is targeted for completion in late 1996.

Photo courtesy of Mirror Lake Carnegie Library

Mirror Lake
Carnegie Library

280 Fifth Street North
St. Petersburg, Florida
33701

Dedication: 1915

Architecture: Beaux-Arts

New Port Richey Public Library
New Port Richey, Florida

Cleveland, Ohio resident, Dr. Elroy McKendree Avery founded the New Port Richey Public Library in 1919 with the donation of his collection of several thousand volumes. The library, then known as The Avery Library and Historical Society, opened on April 10, 1920, in the Snell Building on Main Street. The City of New Port Richey took over the library in 1925. After the depression, it operated the library out of the Municipal Building at 133 Main Street until 1963 when New Port Richey built a new library facility. The City Hall moved into the 1926 Pierce Elementary School located near the library. A 1966 addition to the library included an auditorium and reading room.

In 1987 the City Council authorized a renovation and expansion program for the City Hall and Library. West Palm Beach-based Gee and Jensen Engineers-Architects-Planners, Inc. designed a 39,000-square-foot complex encompassing a new 24,000-square-foot City Hall and a 15,320-square-foot library in the former Pierce Elementary School. Plans incorporated gutting of the interior of the school building while preserving the three red brick walls and architectural styling. The building that housed the old library became the new City Hall after renovation and the library moved to temporary quarters from 1989 to 1991 until the former Pierce Elementary School building was readied for library use.

The architectural plans combined the two community buildings into a linked complex. The grand opening of the new City Hall took place in July 1990 and the new library was dedicated in May 1991. In memory of the library's founder, the New Port Richey Library houses the Avery Conference Room.

Photo courtesy of Denise Robin Gogola, New Port Richey Public Library

New Port Richey Public Library

5939 Main Street
New Port Richey, Florida
34652

Dedication: 1926 as
Pierce Elementary
School

Rededication: 1991 as
New Port Richey Public
Library

Architecture: American
Vernacular

Newark Public Library

5 Washington Street
Newark, New Jersey
07101

Dedication: 1901

Architecture: Italian
Renaissance

Photo courtesy of Jean-Rae Turner

Newark Public Library

Newark, New Jersey

Belief in the importance of books and knowledge in Newark dates back to 1666 when Newark's first settlers brought over 800 books with them on their migration from Connecticut. Later, in 1847, several citizens organized the Newark Library Association as a stock company. The Association collected $15,000 at $25 per share. Member dues were assessed at $1 for three months or $3 for the year.

Voters approved the establishment of a Free Public Library in 1887. Two years later the Board of Trustees leased the renovated Newark Library Association building at West Park near Broad Street and opened to the public with 10,000 books selected from the Association's collection.

Excavation on the present building began on March 14, 1898, the laying of the cornerstone took place on January 26, 1899, and the Newark Public Library was dedicated at a ceremony in the Library's Hall on March 14, 1901.

The Philadelphia architectural firm of Rankin and Kellogg designed a dignified four-story Italian Renaissance structure to incorporate the library, a museum, a lecture hall and an exhibit gallery. An excellent example of Italian Renaissance, the building's exterior texture lightens from level to level, with deeper cuts on the lower levels. The monumental reading room on the second floor covered the entire width of the front of the building facing Washington Street and featured nine large arched windows, a high ornamented ceiling, and massive fireplaces at either end.

Renovation of the library began with Centennial Hall reopening in late 1987. It is a prime meeting and reception center for Newark. In recent years, the library opened two new rooms in the Main Library: the African-American Room and the Sala Hispanoamericana. Committed to fulfilling its role of serving the city's citizens, the Newark Public Library has continued to evolve as the city itself has changed.

Lewis J. Ort Library

Frostburg State
University
Frostburg, Maryland
21532

Completion: 1975

Dedication: 1990 as the
Lewis J. Ort Library

Architecture:
Contemporary

Photo courtesy of Frostburg State University Media Relations

Lewis J. Ort Library

Frostburg, Maryland

The ultramodern five story brick veneer and glass Lewis J. Ort Library on the Frostburg State University campus in Frostburg, Maryland was completed in 1975 at a cost of $4.5 million. However, dedication of the facility to Lewis J. Ort did not occur until October 28, 1990. Mr. Ort is a prominent community member and worldwide philanthropist having built hospitals, orphanages, nurses' residences and medical centers around the world. In addition, he has aided in fund raising for a myriad other charitable projects ranging from the Salvation Army to an electrical generating plant in India.

Mr. Ort is the beneficiary of many awards for his contributions to mankind including the Bishop Fulton J. Sheen Plaque, the Imperial Shrine Crystal Bowl and the first-ever Frostburg State University Medallion.

Architect Emil Kish employed a contemporary style flat-roofed structure with distinctive arches at the outside edges of an arcade to give the building a unique look while maintaining a tie to the smaller Romanesque arches found at the entrance of Old Main, the first building on campus and built in 1899.

Since Frostburg State University is the only Maryland public four year institution west of Baltimore, its Lewis J. Ort Library is also open to the public in the surrounding communities.

Pack Memorial Library

Asheville, North Carolina

Dedicated in July 1926, the four-story Pack Memorial Library represents an excellent example of the Second Renaissance Revival style of public building. Pack Square figured prominently in native son Thomas Wolfe's novels, "Look Homeward Angel" and "You Can't Go Home Again."

Designed by New York library architect Edward L. Tilton, the Pack Memorial Library featured symmetrically arranged elevations faced with white Georgia marble and ornamented with a low-relief classical cornice. The three-story arched entrance drew light into the library. Tilton designed the library around a unique central stack core which virtually eliminated any rearrangement of space as library services changed.

A $5,000 donation from Charles Lathrop Pack in memory of his father, George Willis Pack, provided money for new books. In addition, Charles L. Pack's two sisters donated $1,000 each toward book acquisition.

Tilton called the architectural style appropriate for the building since it recalled the era when learning reawakened after the long dormancy during the Middle Ages. Bas-reliefs by Danish sculptor Albert Bertel Thorwaldsen depicted Alexander's triumphant entrance into Babylon in his chariot driven by the Genius of Victory. The original frieze was executed in 1812 for the Quirinal Palace in Rome.

Pack Memorial Library housed the O'Henry memorial library in honor of another Asheville author, W.S. Porter, whose grave is in Asheville's Riverside Cemetery. The structure served as Asheville's main library from 1926 until 1978. The new library is located several blocks west of the 1926 building on 67 Haywood Street. After more than a decade of vacancy, the 1926 Pack Memorial Library was renovated in 1992 to house the Asheville Art Museum.

The Asheville Art Museum (Pack Memorial Library) represents an excellent example of how a "Cultural Gem" was recycled to be yet another gem for its citizens.

Photo courtesy of North Carolina Collection, Pack Memorial Library

Pack Memorial Library

(Now houses the
Asheville Art Museum)
South Pack Square
Asheville,
North Carolina 28801

Dedication: 1926

Rededication: 1992 as
Asheville Art Museum

Architecture: Second
Renaissance Revival

Harriette Person Memorial Library

Port Gibson, Mississippi

The initial session of Mississippi's Legislature granted Mississippi's first library charter to the Mississippi Literacy and Library Company of Gibson Port in 1818. After fifteen years of inactivity, the Mississippi Library Association resurrected itself in 1858 but probably fell victim to the War between the States.

Miss Harriette Person formed a Port Gibson subscription library in 1914 after spending the summer in Chautauqua, New York and conferring with the head of the Chautauqua Library School. The library opened in the office of Mr. J. Martin Magruder, Circuit Clerk, and charged dues of $1 per year.

The library moved to the Person Building in 1916 with Miss Person as librarian. Clairborne County and the city of Port Gibson started contributing to the library's operation in 1927 and 1928, respectively, and the library became the Port Gibson County Public Library.

In 1934 the library moved to the second floor of the Irvin Russell Memorial Building. Miss Harriette Person served the library for twenty-one years and after her death in 1934, the library was renamed in her memory. The library occupied the first floor of the Russell Building from 1949 until it was closed for renovation in 1991.

That same year, the Clairborne County Board of Supervisors purchased an historic building in the Main Street district of Port Gibson. Belinda Stewart Architects renovated the attractive red brick structure as the new home of the Harriette Person Memorial Library. To be sure, Miss Harriette Person's aim of "establishing a little library, growing with the years and finding an honorable place in the town's history" has been achieved.

Photo courtesy of Billie G. Jones

Harriette Person Memorial Library

606 Main Street
Port Gibson, Mississippi
39150

Dedication: 1991 as
Harriette Person
Memorial Library

Architecture: American
Commercial

Pope Memorial Library
Danville, Vermont

The library movement in Danville, Vermont originated in 1864 with the establishment of the Danville Agricultural Library Association. In 1879 after the demise of the earlier Association, the Ladies Library Association raised money for books and opened a library in space provided in the shop of the local shoemaker, Mr. Saunders.

The library moved a number of times before settling in 1885 in a small brick building purchased for $400, $50 of which was donated by the building's owner, the Honorable Bliss Nash Davis. In 1886 a fire devastated Danville's business section, including the library, but not before the ladies filled their aprons with books and carried them off to safety. Later, news of the fire reached Mrs. Charles Pope of Chicago, who responded with a donation of money for a new library in memory of her husband, a native of Danville.

Architect Marshall Morrill designed a delightful wooden building adorned with diminutive Ionic pilasters around the window frames and dental molding below the roof line. More than a dozen years later, Mrs. Pope donated funds to have hardwood floors laid in the library.

A 1978 addition, financed in part by former librarian Mrs. Annie Currier, houses a children's room. The architect was Tom Fresbee Fulton and the work was performed by the White Brothers. A 1989 donation from Emerson Lang resulted in the installation of a new Palladian window in the reading room. Renovations for the library's centennial in 1990 readied the library for another century of service to the community.

Photo courtesy of Gary Thornton

Pope Memorial Library

On the Green
Danville, Vermont
05828

Dedication: 1890

Architecture: Classical
Revival

Portsmouth Public Library

Portsmouth, Virginia

Private libraries served Portsmouth in the nineteenth century and far into the twentieth century. The Student's Club, a private women's reading and study group, organized a library in 1914 and located it in one room behind the 1846 Court House. Although administered by the City of Portsmouth, the library was owned by the Student's Club and operated on a "whites only" basis.

In the 1940s a black church started a lending library, later taken over by Portsmouth as the Portsmouth Community Library. Portsmouth continued to be served by the private library until 1962 when two African Americans sued the Student's Club Board to admit blacks to the library. One of them, Dr. James Holley, later became Mayor of Portsmouth while the other, Dr. Hugo Owens, became Vice-Mayor of neighboring Chesapeake.

Consolidating of the public library and community library staff and making the library a city department resolved the issue. The Old Post Office, built in 1908 of brick and cut stone, was acquired for one dollar and housed the newly combined library. Renovation of the building in 1963 preserved the original architectural details and won the Virginia Chapter of American Architects Award that year. Glen Yates and Kirk Berkeley were the renovation architects. The building features six large Ionic columns supporting a roofline balustrade and large rounded top facade windows.

The library now serves as headquarters for a four library system. The building is listed in the official guide to historic buildings in Virginia.

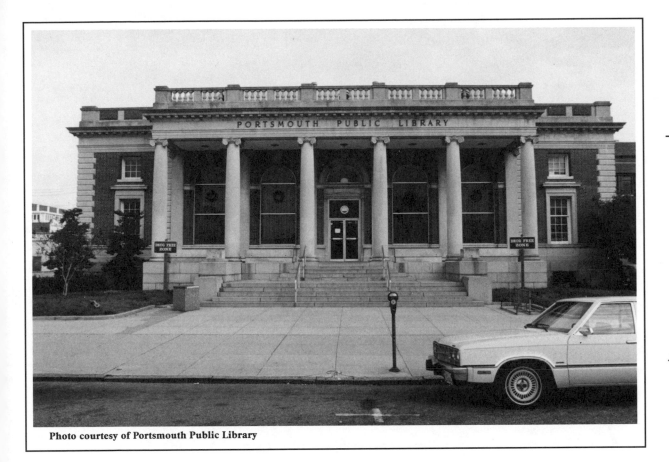

Photo courtesy of Portsmouth Public Library

Portsmouth Public Library

601 Court Street
Portsmouth, Virginia
23704

Dedication: 1908 as
United States Post
Office

Rededication: 1963 as
Portsmouth Public
Library

Architecture: Classical
Revival

Princeton Public Library

2 Town Hall Drive
Princeton,
Massachusetts 01541

Dedication: 1883

Architecture: Chateau

Photo courtesy of Phyllis Booth

Princeton Public Library
Princeton, Massachusetts

The Princeton Public Library collection derives from the union of the library collections of three different organizations: the Ladies Reading Society, the Princeton Agricultural Society and Princeton's Law Library. They came together after Edward A. Goodnow, a native of Princeton and a wealthy Worcester merchant and banker, donated monies for a town library in 1882.

Worcester architect Stephen C. Earle combined Milford, Massachusetts rose granite with Longmeadow brownstone for the exterior walls of the Goodnow Memorial Building, now known as the Princeton Public Library. Black Monson, Maine slate covered the roof while local granite provided the structure's underpinning. The western half of the building comprised a schoolhouse with separate entrances for boys and girls.

The Chateau architecture contains German elements such as the clock tower and Richardsonian elements such as the heavy stone work and recessed entry.

Entrance to the library was achieved through a 70-foot-high clock tower which struck the hours on a thousand pound Meneely bell and inscribed with "Goodnow Memorial Building-Knowledge is Power." The main room features a 25-foot-high arched ceiling finished with ash ribs. A terra cotta fireplace and stained glass adorn the ash furnished reading room. Over the fireplace mantle rests a life-size white Italian marble medallion of Mr. Goodnow set in Spanish marble. Near the entrance, a memorial tablet carved in African onyx is dedicated to Mr. Goodnow's family. Norcross Brothers of Worcester performed the construction and P. A. Butler of Boston did the frescoing.

Providence Public Library
Providence, Rhode Island

The Providence Public Library accepted its charter in 1874 and opened its first library to the public in 1878 in a room at the Butler Exchange. Two years later the library moved into the ground floor of a three-story building of the English and Classical School where it resided for approximately twenty years. Beginning in 1889 Providence made an appropriation each year to help support the library.

During the winter of 1896-97 library officials considered scaling back plans for the proposed new library since donations were not meeting expectations. Three gifts from John Nicholas Brown totaling nearly $270,000 rectified the situation and design and construction proceeded with the Providence Public Library dedication taking place on March 15, 1900. The total cost amounted to $475,000 including $88,000 spent to purchase five lots.

Sansovino's library of Venice's St. Mark's Square and the Library of Saint Genevieve in Paris influenced Providence architects Stone, Carpenter & Willson to design an Italian Renaissance structure to rival those of Europe. The 1900 Providence Public Library's granite base supports soft grey Roman brick accented with Indiana limestone. Its low hipped copper roof features detailed ornamentation.

Sweeping staircases lead up to a terrace adorned with a massive stone balustrade. A triple archway forms the main entrance and supports an overhead balustrade. Inside, mosaic tile, "Pavanazzo marble" walls and columns and exquisite plasterwork add elegance to function.

In 1953 an art deco addition was completed and a major renovation of the two buildings took place between 1984 and 1988. The Providence Public Library was placed on the National Register of Historic Places in 1983.

Photo courtesy of Jean Duffy, Providence Public Library

Providence Public Library

225 Washington Street
Providence, Rhode Island 02903

Dedication: 1900

Architecture: Italian Renaissance

Roddenbery Memorial Library

320 North Broad Street
Cairo, Georgia 31728

Dedication: 1964

Architecture:
Classical Revival

Photo courtesy of Randy Wind, Cairo Messenger

Roddenbery Memorial Library
Cairo, Georgia

The first library in Cairo, Georgia originated as the Cairo Public Library federally funded under the WPA Library Project in 1939. Its 210 books (nearly half on loan from the Georgia Library Commission) were located in a hallway over the city fire station. Later, the library moved across the street into a storefront and received funding from three local government agencies: the city of Cairo, Grady County and the public school system.

In 1944 the Roddenbery family, owners of a local hardware store and the famous W.B. Roddenbery Company, Inc. (pickles and syrup), made arrangement for in-kind donation of material and funds for construction of a new library building. However, actual construction of the library was delayed due to a scarcity of building materials as a result of World War II. Two decades passed before the Roddenbery Memorial Library became a reality, just before the hardware store went out of business in 1964.

Architect Richard V. Richard of Albany, Georgia employed the Classical Revival style with slender Ionic columns and half circle arches to create a feeling of antebellum splendor carried into the interior hallway. An inner courtyard contains several memorial gardens and a brick pathway leading to an outdoor story-telling area. In 1986 state monies supplemented funds raised by local efforts to double the library's space to 18,000-square feet. Architect Frank McCall of Moultrie, Georgia designed the addition to blend in with the original pink brick building and upgraded the interior walls with crown molding.

Rosenberg Library

Galveston, Texas

Swiss emigrant, Henry Rosenberg, bequeathed an endowment for a free public library to the people of Galveston when he died in 1893. In addition, Rosenberg funded free lectures "...upon practical, literary and scientific subjects and such other incidents to a great public library as may be conducive to the improvement, instruction and elevation of the citizens of Galveston...."

The Rosenberg Library Association received a charter from the State of Texas in 1900 and purchased a plot in the center of the city. Eames and Young of St. Louis won the architectural competition and designed a three-story Italian Renaissance structure of brick, stone and terra cotta ornamentation.

Above the Llano County, Texas gray granite rest layers of buff Bedford, Indiana limestone with exterior face brick of light gray. Cream-white, semi-glazed terra cotta embellishes the areas surrounding doors, windows, entablature and arches. Tiger heads line the cornice and each window gable is adorned with a book and scroll. Next to the lower part of the entablature, large decorative panels carry the names of thirteen noted authors such as Homer, Shakespeare, Milton, Schiller and Longfellow.

The pitched portion of the roof is covered with green tile. Inside, on the main floor, Italian marble highlights mantles, vestibule walls and wainscoting of the corridors and stairways.

The Moody Wing, funded principally with a donation from the Moody Foundation, was added in 1971. Architect Thomas M. Price of Galveston blended the addition to the new structure using travertine marble with textured concrete trim and green roof tiles, which closely match the 1904 roof and were made by the original manufacturer. A unique tile mosaic, with varying shades of grey, black and white, rises above the new entrance to unite the Italian Renaissance structure with its more contemporary addition.

Photo courtesy of Rosenberg Library

Rosenberg Library

2310 Sealy Avenue
Galveston, Texas 77550

Dedication: 1904

Architecture: Italian
Renaissance/
Contemporary Addition

Scranton Public Library
Scranton, Pennsylvania

The Scranton Public Library (Albright Memorial Building) resides on the original Albright homestead at the intersection of North Washington and Vine Streets. The heirs of Joseph Jacob Albright and Elizabeth Sellers Albright donated the land and pledged $50,000 to $75,000 in 1890 for the purpose of constructing a suitable building for a public library to benefit the citizens of Scranton and vicinity.

Buffalo architects Green & Wicks patterned the structure after the French Renaissance style of the Musee de Cluny in Paris. The "suitable" building came in at a final cost of $125,000 as evidenced by the stature of the building and its exquisite appointments. The dedication took place on May 25, 1893.

The exterior of the building consists of a warm grey Indiana limestone over a base of brown Medina stone. The steep roof is covered with black Spanish tiles and adorned with twelve dormer gables upon which are carved symbols of notable book makers. Continuing this motif, the tall windows are leaded with stained glass designs representing crests or bookmarks used by the first printers. Ornate grille work and intricate stone carvings unify the exterior.

Inside, quartered oak, marble mosaic and three marble fireplaces accent the reading and reference rooms. On the second floor, six columns of Mycean marble support a high, barrel-vaulted ceiling. Two bronze tablets were presented to the city at the library's fortieth anniversary. One commemorates the first librarian, Henry James Carr, while the other tablet perpetuates the memory of the library building's donors and the homestead site.

Photo courtesy of Jim Davis, Guy Cali Associates

Scranton Public Library

Albright Memorial
Building
500 Vine Street
Scranton, Pennsylvania
18509

Dedication: 1893

Architecture: French
Renaissance/Chateau

Shreve Memorial Library
Shreveport, Louisiana

Shreveport is adept at adjusting to the times and the demands of creative building utilization. The first Shreveport library, a people's library, was operated by a group of local women and located in the court house building. Voters turned down a 1903 attempt to establish a Carnegie Library but after World War I did approve a bond issue that contained a provision for a $265,000 library appropriation.

Architect J.P. Annan modeled the library after a luxurious Italian villa in creating a Renaissance Revival structure built at 400 Edwards Street. When the library shifted to its present quarters in the old Federal Building in 1980, the Chamber of Commerce and the Shreveport Downtown Development Authority moved into the vacated library building.

Plans for the original 1912 building and 1931 addition were prepared under the direction of the Supervising Architect of the U.S. Treasury Department. The Renaissance Revival building features arched limestone and stuccoed brick, a low hipped red tile roof, Doric pilasters with decorative cornice and casement windows with terra cotta trim. The 1931 expansion added a fourth floor.

Architects Walker and Walker preserved the interior lobby marble columns and arched ceilings in the 1978 renovation. The building has been placed on the National Register of Historic Places. Shreve Memorial Library operates nineteen branches and two bookmobiles. It houses special collections in genealogy, government documents, petroleum/geology and rare books.

Photo courtesy of Harry Simmons

Shreve Memorial Library

424 Texas Street
Shreveport, Louisiana
71120

Dedication: 1912 as the
Federal Building

Rededication: 1980 as
Shreve Memorial
Library

Architecture:
Renaissance Revival

Union County Carnegie Library

300 East South Street
Union,
South Carolina 29379

Dedication: 1905 as
Carnegie Free Library

Rededication: 1985 as
Union County Carnegie
Library

Architecture: Greek
Revival

Photo courtesy of Gail E. Agett

Union County Carnegie Library

Union, South Carolina

The early predecessor to today's Union County Carnegie Library dates back to 1803 and the private Union Library Society. In early 1898, the Every Tuesday Club pressed for a public library. The editor and publisher of the "Progress" newspaper corresponded with Andrew Carnegie, resulting in a $10,000 Carnegie library construction grant in 1903 and distinguishing Union as the first recipient of a Carnegie Grant in the State of South Carolina.

The Charlotte, North Carolina architectural firm of Wheeler & Runge designed the 1905 Carnegie Free Library using yellow brick and red mortar to give the building a distinctive Greek Revival look. Terra cotta ornamentation over the windows, Ionic entrance columns, dual typanums (triangular pediments) adorned with scrollwork and a large dome make this library one of a kind. Stained glass over the entrance doors and a stained glass skylight surrounded by ornamental ceiling tiles provide additional unique touches.

With the help of a dedicated librarian, Miss Cornelia Sartor, the Rotary Club of Union and the Works Progress Administration, the Carnegie Free Library struggled through difficult years. The 1966 merger of the Carnegie Free Library and the Union County Traveling Library made available funds from both the county and the state to renovate and expand in order to meet the needs of Union County citizens. The merger created the Union County-City Public Library, later shortened to Union County Carnegie Library.

A 1985 renovation and addition headed by F. Earle Gaulden of Craig, Gaulden & Davis, Architects, Inc. preserved the integrity of the Union County Carnegie Library while tripling the gross square footage available for library use. The Union County Carnegie Library is on the National Register of Historic Places as part of the South Street Historic District.

Samuel H. Wentworth Library

Center Sandwich,
New Hampshire 03227

Dedication: 1915

Architecture: Gothic
with Tudor Influence

Photo courtesy of Samuel H. Wentworth Library

Samuel H. Wentworth Library
Center Sandwich, New Hampshire

The Sandwich and Moultonborough Social Library obtained its incorporation from an Act of the Legislature in 1800. Ten years later the Legislature chartered the Sandwich Social Library. In the early 1820s the Sandwich Cooperative Library formed. The Sandwich Library Association organized in the mid-1880s and was privately managed, meeting at private residences. It evolved into a large group known as Sandwich Free Public Library. The first Free Library building opened in 1899 in a small wood frame structure, later known as the Masonic Hall.

Upon his death in 1912 Samuel H. Wentworth, a former resident and Boston attorney, bequeathed $17,000 to the town for the purpose of erecting a new library building. In addition, summer resident J. Randolph Coolidge of the Boston architectural firm of Coolidge and Carlson, which was hired to prepare the building plans, donated monies to the town to cover the cost of the architectural fees. Design consideration had to be given to Wentworth's stipulation that the building be as fireproof as possible. Coolidge and Carlson responded with a Gothic structure constructed of fieldstone and topped with a distinctive red tile roof. The structure exhibits a Tudor influence with its use of wood beams and wide windows.

The library benefited from the wartime efforts of one of its summer residents who arranged for English children to be taken into homes in Montclair, New Jersey, her winter residence. Her friends established the Helen Barrett Speers Memorial Committee, which purchased books about the United States to be sent to England and books about the British Isles or by British authors to be donated to the Montclair and Sandwich Libraries.

Wentworth generosity exhibited itself again in 1969 upon the death of Maude Smith Wentworth, widow of Joseph Wentworth, making effective the second part of his will leaving approximately $300,000 for the support, benefit, and upkeep of the Samuel H. Wentworth Library. The new funds permitted the addition of a two-story wing at the rear of the building in 1972, doubling the library capacity.

Wilmington Library
Wilmington, Delaware

Evidence of earlier subscription and circulation libraries exist but the official library movement in Wilmington began with the issuance by the Delaware General Assembly of a charter to The Library Company of Wilmington in 1788. It operated as a subscription library with members paying an annual fee and contributing funds for the purchase of books. Over the years, the Library Company absorbed other reading groups and in 1859 a merger with the Young Men's Association for Mutual Improvement resulted in a name change to The Wilmington Institute.

Industrialist William Poole Bancroft's generous gift of $20,000 retired the Institute's debt in 1893 on the condition that a free library be established. The Wilmington Institute Executive Committee voted to convert to free library status in 1893 and opened to the public from a renovated building in 1894 as the Wilmington Institute Free Library. Proceeds from the sale of the Institute's library building, a $245,000 donation from Pierre S. duPont and a seven-day campaign which raised more than $325,000 by popular subscription funded the purchase of property and construction of the new Wilmington Institute Free Library, dedicated in 1923.

Architects Klauder, Tilton and Githens designed a Beaux-Arts structure blended with Ionic and Corinthian elements. Du Pont Engineering Company acted as the general contractor. The American Institute of Architects awarded their Medal of Monumental and Government Buildings to the architects of the Wilmington Institute Free Public Library in 1925.

The facade of the building is rich in symbolic detail. Unique attributes include fluted Ionic columns between the main windows, supporting an elaborate cornice and an intricate polychromatic terra cotta frieze with stylized sphinxes of classical tradition representing learning, knowledge and erudition. The interior follows a palace arrangement with a central top-lighted atrium. Interior black Doric columns adorned with red and cream colored Pompeiian capitals reside on the first floor while yellow Ionic columns enhance the second floor.

Photo courtesy of The Wilmington Library

Wilmington Library

**Tenth & Market Streets
Wilmington, Delaware
19801**

Dedication: 1923

Architecture: Beaux-Arts

III. Plains and Midwestern Region

Anadarko Community Library

215 West Broadway
Anadarko, Oklahoma
73005

Dedication: 1925 as Roy
Hall Chevrolet
Dealership

Rededication: 1991 as
Anadarko Community
Library

Architecture: American
Commercial

Photo courtesy of the Anadarko Daily News

Anadarko Community Library

Anadarko, Oklahoma

Anadarko, named after the Nadarko Indians, has a rich history, beginning as a trading post and Indian mission in Oklahoma Indian Territory and developing into a full fledged town after the land was opened for settlement on August 6, 1901. The Philomathic Club, the first club for women in Indian Territory, originated in 1899 as a local literary club and proved instrumental in organizing Anadarko's first library.

The initial library collection of several hundred books was placed in a furniture store, before moving to a spare room of the local newspaper, "The American Democrat." The number of volumes increased dramatically when the President of the Philomathic Club, Mrs. C. Ross Hume, arranged for 1,000 books from the Territorial Federation of Women's Clubs as a traveling library service. In addition, the Peoria, Illinois library donated another 250 volumes.

In 1907 Philomathic Club members and members of the Men's Commercial Club joined forces to create the Public Library Association. The library became a free public library in 1913 as a department of municipal government supported by the Anadarko taxpayers. It occupied the third floor of the city hall for 26 years before moving in 1936 to a room in the new Masonic Temple.

Citizens established the Anadarko Community Library Trust in 1989 to raise funds for larger and more convenient library facilities. A combination of government grants, private foundation donations, civic clubs efforts, school children's projects and individual and business contributions made the library dream a reality with over $600,000 raised.

Beck Associates of Oklahoma City converted a circa 1925 red brick car dealership building into an efficient library. Beck left the bowstring trusses and steel beams intact, creating a spacious, open feeling. Beck Associates won the 1991 Best Historic Rehabilitation Project Award from the Oklahoma Department of Commerce and an Honorable Mention Award for Adaptive Reuse from "Commercial Renovation Magazine" in 1991 for the design work on the Anadarko Community Library.

Anita Public Library

Anita, Iowa

Located in Southwest, Iowa, the Anita Public Library serves a community of approximately 1,100 citizens. The original church building was constructed on land provided by the Voorhees family and with $4,500 in funds made available by the J.F. Wills estate and donations from church members.

The Christian Science Church donated the structure to the town of Anita in September 1963 with the stipulation that it always be used as a library. The town allocated $11,000 for remodeling and equipping the new library.

Cottage in design, the Anita Public Library exhibits the warmth of a small country cottage. The lot is surrounded by a low stone wall and shrubbery nestles close to the building's foundation. The library itself is built from multicolored cobblestones from the Frank Barber farm north of Anita. Its tall cobblestone chimney separates the twin peaks of the main rooms. Attractive green stained glass fills the panes of the rounded arch window frames.

Inside, large beams and rafters enhance and strengthen the line of cathedral ceilings. Wooden-pegged oak planks form the flooring in this delightful library. A large collection of art is available on loan to patrons. What a wonderful place to spend a few quiet hours.

Photo courtesy of Anita Tribune

Anita Public Library

812 Third Street
Anita, Iowa 50020

Dedication: 1931 as
Christian Science
Church

Rededication: 1963 as
Anita Public Library

Architecture: Cottage

Beatrice Public Library

100 North 16th Street
Beatrice, Nebraska
68310

Dedication: 1991

Architecture:
Contemporary

Photo courtesy of Wayne Price, Beatrice Daily Sun

Beatrice Public Library

Beatrice, Nebraska

Beatrice Public Library skillfully blends the old with the new, incorporating characteristics of the original Carnegie Library (1904) with the technological requirements designed to serve patrons of the 21st century. Since 1893 the Beatrice Public Library has called three places home: The U.S. Post Office (from 1893 to 1903), the Carnegie Building (from 1904 to 1991) and its present location.

Designed by Gary Bowen of the Omaha architectural firm of Bahr Vermeer and Haecker, the Beatrice Public Library won the highest award given by the Nebraska Chapter of the American Institute of Architects in 1992 and a special award from the Masonry Institute in 1992 for the brickwork. "Progressive Architecture" also featured the library's floor plan in its April 1994 issue.

A unique brick mural at the entrance depicts major buildings in the area (including the Carnegie Library) and trees on the site. A window-seat reading area and two courtyards (one planted in wildflowers and prairie grasses and the other a shrubrose garden) bring the indoors and outdoors into close contact with library patrons. The site originally held the home of the owner of the internationally recognized nursery (Sonderegger Nurseries) and the landscaping and library layout were designed to preserve many mature trees on the property. This allowed designation of the library as a Nebraska Arboretum site in 1992.

Native Nebraskan George Lundeen's limited edition sculpture, "Storybooks" graces the library's grounds as a gift from the Cook family in honor of the contributions of Betty C. Cook to the Beatrice Public Library.

Bentonville Public Library

Bentonville, Arkansas

Bentonville's historic Massey Hotel served as headquarters for the Bentonville Public Library twice. The Northwestern Arkansas community's first library opened its doors on November 11, 1918, operating out of the East room of the Massey Hotel. However, the venture proved short lived. Due to lack of funds and inability to pay a librarian and people failing to return borrowed books, the library soon closed. Citizens later revived the library and it moved three times before returning to the Massey Hotel Building in 1979, this time occupying the entire lower level. Business offices occupy the upper floors.

Listed on the National Register of Historic Places, the Massey Hotel's Renaissance Revival style utilizes eight round cast-stone Romanesque columns with stylized acanthus leaf caps to support the wraparound porch. The prominent three-story architectural landmark served Bentonville as a commercial site for over 80 years. Businesses that operated out of the hotel included a train ticket office, barber shop, radio station, and bus station. The Massey Hotel was constructed in 1910 at a cost of $40,000. It replaced the 1840 Eagle Hotel, which served as the Civil War headquarters of General Siegal.

Fire devastated the roof of the Massey Hotel in 1965 and the Walton family (Bentonville is home to Wal-Mart Stores, Inc.) came to the rescue with a beautiful restoration.

Photo courtesy of Bentonville Public Library

Bentonville Public Library

**Massey Building
125 West Central
Bentonville, Arkansas
72712**

**Dedication: 1910 as
Massey Hotel**

**Rededication: 1979 as
Bentonville Public
Library
(Lower level of building)**

**Architecture:
Renaissance Revival**

A.H. Brown Public Library

Mobridge, South Dakota

The library movement began in Mobridge in the early nineteen twenties. The local library trustees purchased two lots with anticipation of receiving a Carnegie Grant for library construction. Unfortunately, after the onset of World War I, Carnegie Grants ceased for new projects.

In 1928 local businessman A.H. Brown offered to build and donate a library building on his own lots in exchange for the lots purchased earlier for the anticipated library. Like Carnegie, Brown also stipulated that the city be responsible for the maintenance of the library building and in the event that the building ceased to function as a library, it would revert back to Brown or his heirs. The trustees accepted the offer, making Brown the first individual in South Dakota to donate a library building to a city.

Architect George Fossum of Aberdeen, South Dakota designed the 1929 structure incorporating seven architectural styles. Prominent features include a Classical influenced entrance, a tiled roof and Dutch-styled gables. The library is listed as an historical landmark.

A 1966 fire caused smoke and water damage but the building remained sound and has been restored. The A.H. Brown Public Library exterior remains the same as the day it was built (with the exception of a new door).

Photo courtesy of A.H. Brown Public Library

A.H. Brown Public Library

521 North Main Street
Mobridge, South Dakota
57601

Dedication: 1929

Architecture: Eclectic

The Brumback Library

Van Wert, Ohio

Dedicated on January 1, 1901, the Brumback Library was constructed with funds bequeathed to Van Wert County by former Van Wert banker/businessman John Sanford Brumback for the purpose of building a free public library. Mr. Brumback's will directed that a sufficient sum from his estate be devoted to the erection and furnishing of a library building as a free gift if Van Wert county would provide for the library's books and the building's maintenance.

The architecture, designed by D.L. Stine of Toledo, Ohio, combined both Gothic and Romanesque to create a handsome well built structure out of Bedford Indiana blue sandstone. Turreted towers and embellished stone carvings give the library a castlesque appearance while the Ludowici tile roof adds a warm, pleasing touch. A grand Gothic entrance leads to the interior which features marble, tile and oak trim.

A 1917 project converted the basement into the Children's Department. A gift from Miss Ellen Reed and Mr. Orville Reed, grandchildren of Mr. Brumback, permitted the complete renovation of the library in 1991 and the 10,500 square-foot Reed Memorial Addition. The Columbus, Ohio architectural firm of McDonald-Cassell & Bassett perfectly blended the new portion with the unique architectural style and materials of the original library structure.

The Brumback Library and its three branches (located in Convoy, Willshire and Wren) comprise one of the first county libraries established in the United States. The library is governed by a Board of Trustees consisting of two Brumback heirs, two members appointed by the City Council and three appointed by the Van Wert County Commissioners.

The Brumback Library provided the initial inspiration for "Cultural Gems." It is only fitting that we used a photo of the Brumback Library to enhance the front and back covers of this book.

Photo courtesy of Larry Dickerhoof

The Brumback Library

215 West Main Street
Van Wert, Ohio 45891

Dedication: 1901

Architecture: Gothic
and Romanesque

Bucyrus Public Library

200 East Mansfield Street
Bucyrus, Ohio 44820

Dedication: 1906

Architecture: Classical Revival

Photo courtesy of The Shooting Gallery, Bucyrus, Ohio

Bucyrus Public Library

Bucyrus, Ohio

Predecessor to the Bucyrus Public Library, the Memorial Library Association organized in 1894 with the purpose of establishing a library in memory of the Civil War dead. The Association erected Bucyrus' first library in 1895 and proved instrumental in obtaining a $15,000 grant in 1905 from Andrew Carnegie for the present library located on the original site of the 1895 library.

Architect Vernon Redding incorporated a large upstairs hall into the two-story structure to serve as a public meeting place. Four massive Ionic columns support the roof of a classic portico above the library's double door entrance, which sits on an angle to Mansfield and Walnut Streets. Dental molding and snowflake paned windows provide unity to all sides of the building as do the decorative pilasters at the library's corners.

A 1989 renovation and expansion, under the guidance of architects Burris & Behne of Marion, Ohio, added an addition onto the rear of the library. Closely matched brick and architectural design makes the addition nearly indistinguishable from the original Carnegie structure.

Over the years, the Bucyrus Public Library has benefited from a rich tradition of generosity by a number of individual and corporate donors, beginning in 1909 with the $26,000 bequest by Nellie R. Harris as a memorial trust in memory of her father.

Carnegie Library
Redfield, South Dakota

In 1902 Redfield, South Dakota garnered the fourth Carnegie Grant to fund library construction in the State of South Dakota. Overall, Carnegie Grants financed the construction of twenty-five libraries in South Dakota between 1901 and 1917. Of these original twenty-five buildings twenty-three still survive. However, only fifteen of these structures continue to fulfill their intended purpose as public libraries.

At the time of the Carnegie bequest to Redfield, the community (situated in the Eastern third of South Dakota almost equidistant from Aberdeen in the north and Huron in the south) was without library service of any kind. The $10,000 grant enabled the town, with a population around two thousand people, to build a majestic red brick library resting on a tan sandstone foundation.

Architect Maurice Hockman from Watertown, South Dakota turned to Roman Classicism for an impressive sense of grandeur featuring a dome and cupola, stalwart columns with plain capitals and clean lines. The arched window opening in the triangular pediment over the entrance repeats around the exterior of the building to provide unity. The extra arch over the round top windows exhibits a touch of Palladian styling. The interior is generously appointed with rich oak columns and woodwork.

The Carnegie Library in Redfield ranks as the oldest Carnegie building in continuous use as a library in South Dakota. The library recently initiated a perpetual gift fund in order to help with upkeep expenses for the future.

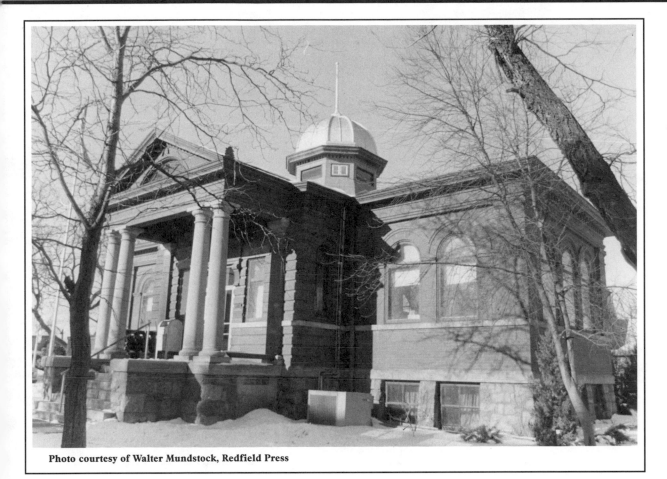
Photo courtesy of Walter Mundstock, Redfield Press

Carnegie Library

Five East Fifth Street
Redfield, South Dakota
57469

Dedication: 1903

Architecture: Roman
Classicism

Carnegie Public Library

219 East Fourth Street
East Liverpool, Ohio
43920

Dedication: 1902

Architecture: Beaux-Arts

Photo courtesy of Carnegie Public Library, East Liverpool, Ohio

Carnegie Public Library
East Liverpool, Ohio

The Trades & Labor Council established the first East Liverpool library in 1896. Local attorney George Travis wrote Carnegie in early 1899 requesting a donation for library construction. Several months later, Carnegie responded with a grant for $50,000, making East Liverpool one of the early recipients of a Carnegie Grant. The facts that Carnegie's uncle and two of his aunts lived in East Liverpool and Andrew had spent time in the city in his youth may have influenced his prompt decision and the amount of the bequest. In comparison, another Ohio city three times East Liverpool's size received a Carnegie Grant for only $37,000 in 1903.

With the help of 20 local businessmen donating $1,000 each, property was secured for the library site at 219 East Fourth Street. Architect Alpheus W. Scott chose the Beaux-Arts style to create an impressive community building. Scott employed buff brick on a sandstone foundation. He embellished the structure with white-glazed terra cotta trim and a variation of a Palladium window over the balustrade. Unique features include a large, tile covered central dome, arched portal and large columns guarding the entrance.

The upper floor of the original library encompassed a public meeting room and a pottery/local history museum. The museum moved across the street in 1972 to form the nucleus of the Ceramics Museum now operated by the Ohio Historical Society. The Carnegie Public Library received designation on the National Register of Historic Places in 1980. Renovation work started in 1992 will preserve this cultural gem for generations to come.

Cary Public Library

255 Stonegate Road
Cary, Illinois 60013

Dedication: 1925 as
Hertz Mansion

Rededication: 1978 as
Cary Public Library

Architecture: Modified
English Tudor

Photo courtesy of Diane R. McNulty, Cary Public Library

Cary Public Library
Cary, Illinois

The current Cary Public Library will soon become history as voters passed a referendum to construct a new library building to serve the community's growing library requirements. The building came to the Village of Cary after years of ownership by several prominent Chicago area names.

In the 1920s John D. Hertz, a founder of the Yellow Cab Company of Chicago and Hertz Rent-A-Car, hired a British architect named Andrews to design a large brick English Tudor mansion for his estate on the outskirts of Cary. The building included an indoor arena for Hertz's show horses and polo ponies.

Otto Schnering, the owner of Curtiss Candy Company, purchased the complex in 1943 and operated his Curtiss Breeding Service from there. In 1968 G.D. Searle and Company, a Chicago area pharmaceutical company acquired the breeding service and property.

Over the years as Cary grew, the complex became the geographical center of the village. In September 1974, G.D.Searle donated the Curtiss arena and surrounding property to the Village of Cary. The library moved into part of the building in 1978 using the trophy wing as the main reading room. It contains a stone fireplace and a cathedral ceiling with rafters. Interestingly, patrons enter the library through the original fodder silo.

When the library moves to its new building, the Village Hall will expand into the trophy wing.

Cattermole Memorial Library

614 Seventh Street
Fort Madison, Iowa 52627

Dedication: 1893

Architecture: Romanesque/Chateau

Photo courtesy of Joe Geren, Daily Democrat

Cattermole Memorial Library

Fort Madison, Iowa

A Southeastern Iowa community with a population under 12,000 appears like one of the least likely places to encounter a medieval looking structure. However, the benefactor and her husband were natives of England.

The Cattermole Memorial Library is unique in another respect as well, representing one of the earliest examples of local philanthropic support for public libraries. The library construction was funded by Elizabeth Cattermole as a memorial to her late husband, Henry, a founder of the German-American Bank in Fort Madison and a force in the local pork packing industry. When Mr. Cattermole died in 1891, he left instructions for his wife to erect a library to serve the city in which they lived for many years. Mrs. Cattermole carried out his wishes and built the library at a cost of $25,000 in 1893.

Hannibal, Missouri architect J.C. Sunderland employed a combined Romanesque/Chateau style with wide arches, brick and stone work, terra cotta trimmings and a slate roof with dormers to convey strength and permanence. The rounded arches are repeated over the doorways and lower windows, unifying the building. The heavy stone work at the base has a Richardsonian influence.

The library's collection includes a number of interesting artifacts such as a sketch of aging Chief Black Hawk which is registered with the Smithsonian Institution in Washington, D.C.

Chandler Public Library
Chandler, Oklahoma

The Chandler Public Library is a good example of recycling buildings for another community purpose. The Chandler City Council formally established a public library for this city of approximately 2,600 people (5,000-6,000 people in area) on February 3, 1987. Soon after, the library moved into the basement of City Hall with books and furnishings provided by the Lincoln County Library, opening to the public in early June 1987.

In 1991 the city agreed to pay $50,000 toward larger facilities if the Library Board could obtain a grant to offset other costs. A "Friends of the Library" was organized and solicited individual, business and organizational donations totaling over $25,000. Coupled with a Title II LSCA grant of $75,000, the donations allowed for the purchase of the first floor of The Clapp-Cunningham Building (also known as the Landmark Building) for $69,000.

Originally built in 1900, the two-story, American Vernacular structure exhibits a Sullivanesque influence with patterned brick work and terra cotta clay embellishment. Built by Wichita, Kansas financier, L.W. Clapp, the building had been restored during 1982-83 using U.S. Secretary of Interior standards for rehabilitation of historic buildings. The building is on the National Register of Historic Places as one of several territorial commerical buildings of Chandler. Over the years, the Clapp-Cunningham Building has housed a bank, dressmaker, general store, other commercial establishments, offices, the Cunningham family's conversion of offices into a hotel and now the Chandler Public Library.

Photo courtesy of Sherman Photography

Chandler Public Library

1021 Manvel Avenue
Chandler, Oklahoma
74834

Dedication: 1900 as
The Clapp Building

Rededication: 1992 as
Chandler Public
Library (first floor)

Architecture: American
Vernacular with
Sullivanesque Influence

Chanute Public Library
Chanute, Kansas

While the Santa Fe Passenger Depot in Chanute, Kansas used to transport people to faraway places, the Chanute Public Library, which now occupies the structure, transports people to new worlds and adventures through its educational and library resources.

The two-story, pressed red brick depot building was constructed in 1903 at a cost of $40,000 by the Lawrence, Kansas firm of W.R. Carter. The Romanesque Revival-influenced structure featured grey trimming, a heavy slate roof, a train tower, ticket office, news stand, large baggage rooms, a lunchroom and separate ladies and gentlemen's waiting rooms. The second story housed the station manager and ten assistants as well as several offices.

A $50,000 expansion in 1917 nearly doubled the depot's size with extensions to the north, south and east ends of the building. The last passenger train departed from Chanute in 1971 and final freight service from the Chanute depot ended in February 1983. The city acquired the building after four years of vacancy and with the aid of public subscription raised $2 million for an historic renovation of the depot. Cable television businessman, Larry Hudson, donated the first $500,000 through his Foundation and later added another $250,000. The Chanute Public Library moved into the partially completed building in August 1992 followed by the Safari Museum in August 1993. A Grand Opening was held on August 28, 1993. The former depot is once again on track as a valuable community resource. The new library replaced the 1906 Carnegie Library which was converted into the Hudson Judicial Center in 1994.

Photo courtesy of Mark Colston

Chanute Public Library

111 North Lincoln, Chanute, Kansas 66720

Dedication: 1903 as Santa Fe Railroad Depot

Rededication: 1993 as Chanute Public Library

Architecture: Train Depot

Chariton Free Public Library

Chariton, Iowa

In the March 27, 1889, city election, the people of Chariton voted yes for a free public library to be established. Later that year, Mayor G.W. Alexander appointed the first library board. Board members Mrs. Victoria Dewey, Mrs. John P. Herrick and Mr. Thomas Gay played instrumental roles in obtaining a $10,000 Carnegie Grant in 1903 and secured an additional $1,000 in 1904 for design changes made "in the interest of durability and convenience."

The Chicago architectural firm of Patton & Miller designed a one-story building constructed of vitrified brick, trimmed with white stone and topped with a tile roof. Quarter sawed golden oak gives the interior a rich luster. Another Chicago firm, Spierling & Linder, performed the fresco work.

The Chariton Free Public Library served as a model, known as the "Chariton Plan," followed with slight variations by Patton and Miller in many of the later Iowa libraries designed by the firm. The Chariton Plan featured a center entrance in the front of the building and typically an interior layout with two wings serving as reading rooms.

The cornerstone was laid by Mrs. Victoria Dewey on April 23, 1904. As noted by the Chariton Leader, "This is the first time we have ever heard of a woman officiating at the formal laying of a cornerstone of any public building. Mrs. Dewey performed her duties in that capacity with dignity and grace." Mrs. Dewey was the mother of Walter Dewey, editor of the Chariton Leader at the time. The dedication of the Chariton Free Public Library took place in November 1904.

A 1992 addition doubled the size of the library at a cost of approximately $850,000. The 1903 circulation desk is still in use today. The new wing (at the rear of the original building in the photograph) perfectly matches the design and material, both inside and outside, of the original Carnegie Library. It represents a textbook example of how to maintain the original architectural integrity of the original structure while meeting the growing needs of the community.

Photo courtesy of Jessie J. Smith, Chariton Newspapers, Inc.

Chariton Free Public Library

803 Braden
Chariton, Iowa 50049

Dedication: 1904

Architecture: Classical Revival

Chisholm Public Library

Chisholm, Minnesota

Chisholm, Minnesota is one of the communities that originally applied for a Carnegie Grant but later rejected the restrictions placed by Carnegie on the library design. Instead, the citizens opted to tax themselves in order to build a library designed to meet the needs of its patrons.

The Chisholm Public Library was constructed from 1913-1914 at the Corner of Lake Street and Third Avenue for a cost of $37,000, including the acquisition of four lots. The brick building employs a number of unique features, including a master staircase leading up to the main library entrance. Doors on either side of the bottom of the main staircase open onto winding stairs, descending to the lower level holding the children's reading area. Ornate pilasters flank either side of the main entrance while an elaborate crest is situated above the doorway. The contractor was Johnson Construction and Engineering Company of Minneapolis. The Board was unanimous in its selection of "Navajo" brick for the exterior at a cost of $24.50.

Reflecting the melting pot of the northern Minnesota Iron Range, the library's early collection of volumes included works in seven languages: Croatian, English, Finnish, Italian, Slovenian, Serbian and Swedish. The building included an auditorium and game room. Numerous small games were purchased to acquaint citizens with "fashionable" games.

The formal dedication took place on May 15, 1914. With the exception of new doors, windows and staircase, the library looks virtually the same as in 1914.

Archibald W. Graham served on the library board for many years. The community's school doctor and a prominent citizen, Dr. Graham, more recently attained notoriety in Burt Lancaster's portrayal of him as Doc "Moonlight" Graham in the popular movie, "Field of Dreams."

Photo courtesy of Chisholm Public Library

Chisholm Public Library

300 West Lake Street
Chisholm, Minnesota
55719

Dedication: 1914

Architecture:
Romanesque Revival

Clinton Township Public Library

Waterman, Illinois

The Clinton Township Public Library began as a reading room in 1904 through the efforts of the Waterman Woman's Club. A club committee solicited books, periodicals and cash contributions to fund and stock the reading room which rented a room above Dean's Drug Store. In 1911 the voters of Clinton Township approved a tax-supported library and elected a library board.

Requests for a Carnegie Grant for construction of a library building were submitted in 1905, 1911 and 1912. On January 31, 1913, Clinton Township received a grant of $3,500. At that time, Clinton Township ranked as the smallest governmental unit in the United States to have obtained approval for a Carnegie library. Voters approved a two-and-a-half-mill tax to support the library maintenance requirement and construct a basement for the proposed library. Local residents pitched in with horse-drawn scoops to dig the basement.

The Chicago architectural firm of Ashby and Sons designed the square brick building and Benjamin Zolper and Sons of Mendota, Illinois constructed the building after a delay due to a brickmakers' strike. The library remains virtually the same as in 1914 with the exception of improvements such as new doors and windows and improved lighting fixtures.

Photo courtesy of Clinton Township Public Library

Clinton Township Public Library

110 South Elm Street
Waterman, Illinois
60556

Dedication: 1914

Architecture: American
Vernacular with Prairie
Influence

Defiance Public Library

Defiance, Ohio

Twenty-five Defiance citizens formed a subscription membership library in December 1867 under the name of the Defiance Library Association. The library holdings resided at a variety of locations over the years from the Clerk of Court office to the Western Union Telegraph office. In 1895 the City of Defiance approved a provision for a municipal library and a mill tax levy to support its operation. The Defiance Library Association donated its books to the municipal library. Carnegie approved a $22,000 library construction grant in November 1903 and later increased the grant amount by another $4,500.

The Defiance Public Library is situated at the west end of historically significant Fort Defiance Park (the site of General Anthony Wayne's Fort Defiance in 1794). Nearby, the former capital of the Miami Indians hosted the largest known "Indian Council Fire" (lighted for all tribes from Hudson Bay to the gulf) for which participating tribes took "a season to arrive."

Architects John Wing and Marshall Mahurin of Fort Wayne, Indiana designed the two-and-a-half-story Gothic structure of red-variegated sandstone quarried at Mansfield, Ohio. The central dome features a stained glass skylight. The rear of the building allows a good view of the Maumee River.

Later additions containing the children's wing on the east and the reference section on the west are built of white Indiana limestone matching the trim of the original structure. The Defiance Public Library achieved National Register of Historic Places status in 1986. When dedicated in 1905, the local newspaper described the Defiance Public Library as "the handsomest library structure in point of architecture, natural surroundings and beautiful interior in the country."

Photo courtesy of William C. Parker

Defiance Public Library

320 Fort Street
Defiance, Ohio 43512

Dedication: 1905

Architecture: Gothic
with Contemporary
Additions

Duluth Public Library

520 West Superior
Street
Duluth, Minnesota
55802

Dedication: 1980

Architecture:
Contemporary

Photo courtesy of Duluth Public Library

Duluth Public Library

Duluth, Minnesota

Duluth residents met at Sargent's Banking House in 1869 to form the Young Men's Library and Literary Association. A reading room on the second floor of a building owned by Colonel Charles H. Graves at 106 West Superior Street served as Duluth's first library. It provided newspapers and popular magazines to dues paying members. After the initial library association faltered, the Ladies Literary Association took hold until an 1889 fire forced it out of business.

In 1890 the first public library opened in Duluth, operating out of the old Masonic Temple Building on the corner of Second Avenue East and Superior Street. Carnegie granted $50,000 in 1899 and later increased his donation by another $25,000 (an additional $45,000 was requested) in order to build the library designed by Duluth architect Adolph F. Rudolph. The 1902 Carnegie Library featured a grand marble stairway with bronze railings leading up to a rotunda with an impressive dome. A stained glass window depicting Minnehaha highlighted the main reading room. Today, the Carnegie Library has been recycled for commercial use.

Designed by architect Gunnar Birkerts of the Birmingham, Michigan firm of Gunnar Birkerts and Associates, the $6.7 million Duluth Public Library reflects Duluth's geographical and economic characteristics. The 330-foot long profile of the library signifies the city stretched out along the shores of Lake Superior. Likewise, its shape resembles the iron ore boats which ply their way into and out of this Great Lakes port city. Birkerts painted a yellow circle on the soffit of the library's forward (East) overhang, as a visual reminder of the bright summer. The new Duluth Public Library was dedicated on June 28, 1980.

Halls Public Library

Halls, Tennessee

Library service began in the small Mississippi River community of Halls, Tennessee in 1956 with the arrival of a bookmobile. The first local library opened in September 1980 in a former medical clinic. Two years later the Tennessee Bicentennial Fund provided the monies to secure the present library building and renovate it for library use.

The Halls Public Library represents an excellent example of recycling older buildings to serve the community in new and innovative ways. Initially a Sinclair Service Station owned and operated by Halls resident, Mr. J.G. "Gid" Milam, the library building enjoys a central location.

Special care was taken to preserve the structure's original Spanish Colonial style architecture during the renovation. The adobe-like walls and red tile trimmed roof give the library a distinctive southwestern flavor in this Western Tennessee town.

In 1984 under the direction of the Memphis architectural firm of James Williamson/Carl Awsumb Architects, the Halls Public Library expanded from 800 square feet to 1,200 square feet. The addition created a reading room in the front of the building, where town residents used to drive their automobiles under the Spanish arch canopy to "fill er up." Funding for this addition was obtained via approval through the Library Service and Construction Act Fund.

The unique renovation of the old Sinclair Service Station into an active community library caught the attention of Tennessee's Secretary of State, Gentry Crowell, who made a special visit to Halls in 1986 to visit the new library.

Photo courtesy of Phillip D. Hurt

Halls Public Library

110 North Church
Street
Halls, Tennessee 38040

Dedication: 1930s as
Sinclair Service Station

Rededication: 1982 as
Halls Public Library

Architecture: American
Venacular with Spanish
Colonial Influence

Hutchinson Memorial Library

228 North High Street
Randolph, Wisconsin
53956

Dedication: 1937

Architecture: Classical/
Moderne

Photo courtesy of The Advance

Hutchinson Memorial Library

Randolph, Wisconsin

The library movement in Randolph, Wisconsin dates back to 1872 with a circulating library in each of the village's drug stores, Addison Lightner's and John Lightner's. In 1906 citizens established a public library in the Mrs. J. Davis Millinery Shop and the village appropriated $50 for its operation. The library moved above the Schatz store in 1914 and to the Cram Building in 1916.

Mary Hutchinson Morris' will named the Village of Randolph as its chief beneficiary, bequeathing the sum of $22,000 and property in 1935 with the request that the money and property be used for the establishment of a free public library.

Milwaukee architects Clas & Clas, Inc. designed the one-story, hipped roof Hutchinson Memorial Library using native light yellow limestone in a random pattern to create a striking, clean appearance. A hanging lantern-style light fixture highlights the recessed double door entrance. Complementary wall-mounted light fixtures adorn either side of the portal. Fluted pilasters flow upward to the entablature inscribed with "Hutchinson Memorial Library." A multi-light transom rests over the double, three-panel wood doors of the entryway.

Due to the location of the donated property, the Hutchinson Memorial Library is located outside of the downtown commerical district, within a residential neighborhood of turn-of-the-century wood and brick homes. The library is listed on the National Register of Historic Places.

Indianapolis-Marion County Public Library

40 East St. Clair Street
Indianapolis, Indiana
46204

Dedication: 1917

Architecture:
Beaux-Arts

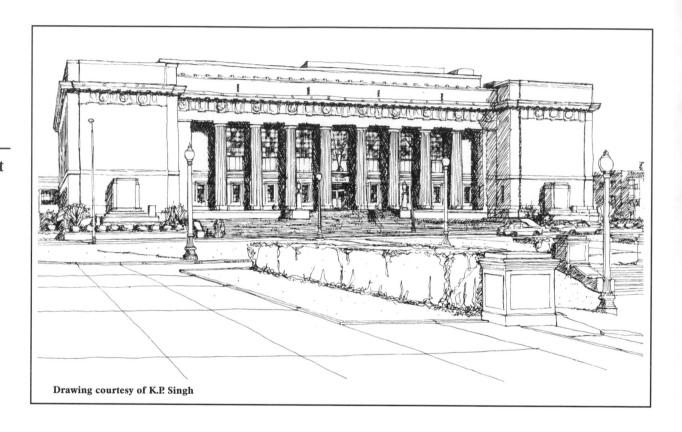

Drawing courtesy of K.P. Singh

Indianapolis-Marion County —— Public Library

Indianapolis, Indiana

Prior to 1873 the private libraries of prominent Indianapolis residents were available to acquaintances and associates. The first free public library came about in response to an impassioned plea in 1868 by the Reverend Hanford A. Edson, pastor of the Second Presbyterian Church, that "...the great want of a city, the deficiency that is really fatal to its character is the want of a public library. No community can be respectable without books...."

The Indianapolis Library Association formed in 1869 as a subscription library, selling shares of stock for $150. In 1871 the Indiana General Assembly passed legislation authorizing tax levies for the support of free libraries.

The Indianapolis Public Library opened in April 1873, located in the High School building. As the need for more space grew, the library moved to the Indianapolis Sentinel Building in 1876. Four years later, it moved to the Alvord House at the southwest corner of Pennsylvania and Ohio Streets. In 1893 Indianapolis built a new Central Library for $200,000 at Ohio and Meridian Streets. Before long, heavy use and a growing collection exceeded the building's capacity.

In 1909 Carnegie approved $100,000 for five Indianapolis branch libraries but the $500,000 in funds for construction of the new main library derived from a 1913 bond issue. Architect Paul Philippe Cret, architect for the Folger Shakespeare Library and the Pan American Union Building in Washington, D.C., designed the structure in Beaux-Arts style. James Whitcomb Riley donated a parcel of land as part of the new library site.

The exterior of the building is Bedford limestone on a base of Vermont granite. Carved stone cornices and impressive Greek columns adorn the structure. Quarter sawed Indiana white oak highlights the interior along with ornamental plaster created on the site and wood and stone carvings. Elegant beauty is found throughout the library, especially in the Main, East and West Reading Rooms. The names of seventy-six literary men and women are inscribed in the stonework above the windows and include Indiana native James Whitcomb Riley.

The library was selected as one of eighteen outstanding architectural achievements to be included in Edward Hoak and Willis S. Church's "Masterpieces of Architecture in the United States," published by Charles Scribner's Sons in 1930. Three years of renovation work was completed in 1987, restoring the library to its former grandeur.

Louisiana Public Library

121 North Third Street
Louisiana, Missouri
63353

Dedication: 1905

Architecture:
Medieval Revival/
Richardsonian
Romanesque

Photo courtesy of Walt Gilbert, Louisiana Press-Journal

Louisiana Public Library

Louisiana, Missouri

Miss Anna Draper, a local book store proprietor and member of the Century Club provided the impetus in 1900 to sponsor a movement to obtain a public library for Louisiana, Missouri. Around the same time, industrialist Andrew Carnegie embarked on his venture of providing construction funds to communities dedicated to building free public libraries for their citizens. After two years of correspondence, Carnegie pledged $10,000 with the stipulations that Louisiana provide a suitable site, elect a Library Board of Directors and pass a tax resolution assuring the library's upkeep.

In short order the mill levy was passed and voters went to the polls with the understanding that each vote cast for the winning site out of six options would donate $1 towards the purchase of that site. The property on the corner of Third and Tennessee won with 3,100 votes and the livery stable owner who occupied the site sold out for $3,000.

Edward Ward received the contract to build the limestone structure for $9,200. The Masons laid the cornerstone on May 4, 1904, the library opened to the public on January 15, 1905, and the formal dedication took place on Washington's birthday, February 22, 1905. The library remains virtually as it did in 1905 with the exception of minor updating of lighting fixtures, the addition of ceiling fans, roof and trim refurbishing and basement renovation for more efficient library use.

The stonework is equal to any found around the country and exhibits a distinctive but inviting feeling. On its 75th anniversary, the library was re-roofed, trim painted, new fixtures installed and front door refinished.

Marion County Public Library

321 Monroe Street
Fairmont, West Virginia
26554

Dedication: 1911 as
United States Post
Office

Rededication: 1942 as
Marion County Public
Library

Architecture:
Classical Revival

Photo courtesy of Dan Gurash

Marion County Public Library

Fairmont, West Virginia

Members of the Women's Christian Temperance Union established Fairmont's first free library in 1892 as a small reading room, offering young men an alternative to frequenting saloons. By 1893 the women purchased a lot at the corner of Fairmont Avenue and First Street for $900. Sale of stock at $10 per share financed the construction of the red brick W.C.T.U. Free Public Library opened in 1896. The name changed to the Fairmont Public Library in 1900 and hard times forced the dissolution of the library in 1920.

The library movement was resurrected in the mid-1920s with cash and book donations from churches, service organizations, professional groups and the schools. A library was established in two rooms of the YMCA on the corner of First Street and Fairmont Avenue in 1926. Once again difficult economic conditions forced the closing of the library in 1937, this time for eight months. In 1939 the Library Committee received approval by the State Legislature for the city library to be taken over and operated as a County Library by the Board of Education, the County Court and City of Fairmont.

The opening of a new Federal Building in 1942 allowed for the purchase of the red brick Old Post Office by the County Court for $17,000, for use as the Marion County Public Library. The 1942 conversion of the building to library use was followed by a complete renovation in 1953. The Fairmont Jr. League's long and generous help contributed to many major changes. It led the community renovation project with work and materials donated by forward looking, dedicated citizens and businesses.

A December 1991 fire resulted in the library being restored again to serve future generations. The village's belief comes thorough clearly, "A library is a good thing."

Dwight T. Parker Public Library

Fennimore, Wisconsin

Since 1849 the Fennimore library collection had been housed in a room at the Methodist Church or at the Old Fennimore House. In 1922 Fennimore banker, Dwight T. Parker, donated the sum of $35,000 for the construction of a library on an "adequate site" to "focus as one of the beautiful points of interest in the City of Fennimore." Upon his death in 1934 Parker's will added a $10,000 trust fund dedicated to the operation of the library. After depletion of the trust fund, Fennimore assumed the library's total cost of operation.

The Dwight T. Parker Public Library in Fennimore, Wisconsin represents an excellent example of the small-scale library construction. Madison, Wisconsin architects Louis Ward Claude and Edward F. Starck incorporated an Italianate theme into the design of the Fennimore library, completed in 1924.

The red brick two-story rectangular building with wide overhanging eaves features a hipped red clay tile roof with a single brick chimney rising through the southeast slope of the roof in the rear of the building. The pedimented frontispiece and coping on the projecting entry are terra cotta. Two sets of three round-headed windows flank each side of the entryway and are adorned with terra cotta colonettes and bracketed sills. Inside, oak moldings and furnishings give a warm feel to the library as does a tile fireplace.

Photo courtesy of Matt Johnson

Dwight T. Parker
Public Library

925 Lincoln Avenue
Fennimore, Wisconson
53809

Dedication: 1924

Architecture: Italianate

Paxton Carnegie Library

254 South Market
Street
Paxton, Illinois 60957

Dedication: 1904

Architecture:
Renaissance Revival

Photo courtesy of Paxton Record

Paxton Carnegie Library

Paxton, Illinois

Prior to 1903 Paxton residents had to depend on the limited resources of private reading rooms for their access to books. The Paxton City Council enacted an ordinance on February 2, 1903, providing for a city property tax to support a public library. Paxton businessman E.B. Pitney led the effort to obtain a Carnegie Grant in the amount of $10,000 which resulted in the laying of the cornerstone in October 1903 and the library dedication on June 27, 1904. The central location plot was purchased with citizen donations totaling $2,000.

Designed by architect Paul O. Moratz of Bloomington, the rectangular stone and brick structure with galvanized iron rotunda was constructed by local builder N.H. Pearson. Moratz designed at least 20 libraries in Illinois, mostly in small towns. The Paxton Carnegie Library's rotunda main reading area sported a marble fireplace while large columns throughout the interior gave an uplifting feeling. Other features included built-in bookstack shelving and an impressive half-circular information and circulation desk. Outside, a pediment graces the main entrance. During the early 1980s, the architectural firm of Severns and Rishling presided over basement renovation to better utilize the library's space.

In 1915 the University of Illinois included photographs of the Paxton Carnegie Library in its display of Illinois Carnegie Libraries at the San Francisco Panama-Pacific International Exposition. Over the years, various organizations such as the Ladies Home Culture Club, the Paxton Woman's Club, the Paxton Junior Woman's Club and the American Legion have been instrumental in generating memorial gift donations to the library.

Clara Lincoln Phelan Memorial Library

Bowman, North Dakota

In June 1913 twenty-one ladies met with the purpose of establishing a library in Bowman, located in the far Southwestern corner of North Dakota, nearly 100 miles from the nearest North Dakota community of any size. The newly formed Library Association received a rent-free room from the Masonic Lodge, situated above the local meat market. Generous donations of a kerosene lamp, coal, kindling, cash and books were also received.

The library moved to a permanent location in November 1915 with the donation of a new library building by J.E. Phelan. Nearly thirty years later, the deed to the Clara Lincoln Phelan Memorial Library was turned over to the Village of Bowman by the Phelan estate on October 13, 1943.

Progress and increased use changed the library over time. The kerosene lamp and fireplace heat gave way to electric lights and gas heat. An addition in 1945 blended well with the original style, following the same graceful roof lines. This addition provided more room for adult nonfiction books and young adult reading space. A 1983 addition doubled the size of the original building and the previous addition was remodeled for workroom/storage/office space and the children's section.

True to its architectural style, the Clara Lincoln Phelan Memorial Library represents a comfortable cottage from which to hide away with a good book or perform some research. Since 1919 the library has been supported on a taxation basis.

Photo courtesy of Lauren Homelvig

Clara Lincoln Phelan Memorial Library

Three First Street West
Bowman, North Dakota 58623

Dedication: 1915

Architecture: Cottage

Phillips County Library

623 Pecan Street
Helena, Arkansas 72342

Dedication: 1891

Architecture: Modified
Second Empire

Photo courtesy of Juanita Milam

Phillips County Library
Helena, Arkansas

The Phillips County Library has always been a focal point for community activities. During its first two decades of existence it also functioned as Helena's Civic Center; frequently being put to use for dances, receptions and women's club meetings. Occasionally, its space was devoted to religious services and school classes. In 1914 for the first time the main room (Library Hall) saw exclusive use as a library.

In 1891 Helena contractors, Raenhart and Simon, built the two and one-half-story building at a cost of $6000. Architect Andrew P. Coolidge designed the 1929 one and one-half-story museum addition located behind the library. Community money-raising efforts that included using Library Hall as a skating rink funded the museum addition.

The museum's collection includes letters from Samuel Clemens (Mark Twain) and General Robert E. Lee. The Phillips County Library was placed on the National Register of Historic Places in 1975 and restored in 1980 through a funding grant from the Department of Arkansas Natural and Cultural Heritage.

A modified example of the Second Empire style, the Phillips County Library features a French mansard roof with paired gable dormers and a facade divided by brick pilasters into three bays. Originally, patrons entered the library via the north bay but construction in 1914 moved the library entrance to its present position in the center of the facade. For many years the library was painted a vibrant pink.

Ponca City Library

515 East Grand Avenue
Ponca City, Oklahoma
74601

Dedication: 1935

Rededication: 1989

Architecture:
Mediterranean

Photo courtesy of Ponca City Library

Ponca City Library

Ponca City, Oklahoma

Women of the Twentieth Century Club of Ponca City, Oklahoma established the Ponca City Library in 1904, only ten years after the founding of the town. At the time, Ponca City's population stood around 2,000. Today, Ponca City boasts in excess of 26,000 residents. The library effort started with fifty volumes located in the back room of a local insurance company office.

In 1908 several years before the discovery of "black gold," Andrew Carnegie provided a $6,500 Grant for the construction of a library in the growing community. With the discovery of oil and the subsequent population explosion exceeding 16,000 people, the town began outgrowing the Carnegie structure by 1920.

In 1934 Ponca City took advantage of a Federal Public Works Administration building program, matching a $100,000 grant with a voter approved bond issue. Ponca City architect George J. Cannon designed an attractive Mediterranean cream and buff brick structure adorned with elaborate terra cotta trim around the windows and portals and two spiral columns with Corinthian capitals supporting the three main entrance arches.

A $1.65 million (nearly one-third raised by private donations) expansion completed in 1989 more than doubled the size of the original building. Howard and Porch, Architects and Engineers of Oklahoma City preserved the unique architectural style of the original structure which was also renovated. The library houses an extensive oriental and western art collection, reflecting the artistry also found in the structure.

Ponca Public Library

203 Second Street
Ponca, Nebraska 68770

Dedication: 1913

Architecture:
Roman Revival

Photo courtesy of Carl Armstrong, Ponca Library Board Member

Ponca Public Library
Ponca, Nebraska

Ponca Public Library owns the distinction of having been the last library approved for a Carnegie construction grant in Nebraska. The steel industrialist and philanthropist approved a $4,500 grant for Ponca's library on April 25, 1911, with the provision that the community maintain the building with tax funds.

The library was built in 1913 of gray sandstone. Located on a hill in the center of town, the library's Roman Revival architecture features a front entrance arch and pilasters. Over the entrance, "Carnegie Library" is engraved into the stone. The building's sleek lines exemplify efficiency. Large windows permit plenty of natural light to enter the reading areas.

An interesting story about the building construction concerns a Mr. Albert Haugan. The young Mr. Haugan was employed to work on the construction of the library. He reported that he was scheduled to sail on the Titanic in 1912 and decided the day before it departed not to travel at that time. His photo, along with other construction workers, hangs in the Ponca Public Library.

The library building has served the less than 900 citizens of this northeastern Nebraska town and several small surrounding communities well over the more than 80 years of its existence.

Prairie Creek Public Library District
Dwight, Illinois

The red brick building housing the Prairie Creek Public Library District in Dwight, Illinois served as a barn (carriage house) on the estate John R. Oughton, one of the founders of the Keeley Institute (for the treatment of alcohol dependency). The 15 acres of grounds were landscaped by the renowned Pittsburgh firm of Elliott and Company. In 1895 Joliet, Illinois architect Julian Barnes renovated a Victorian structure moved to the property. Mrs. Oughton christened their new home, the "Manse."

As a result of a dwindling caseload, during 1929-1930, Oughton converted the Manse into housing for patients and the 50' by 80' barn with slate roof into a gymnasium and recreation facility. The Keeley Institute closed its doors in 1965. James Oughton, Jr., grandson of the original owner, converted the institute into a restaurant and later sold it and adjacent acres to another party. Ownership to the remaining property remained with the Leslie Keeley Company of which Mr. Oughton was President.

The Dwight Public Library owes its origin to the Dwight Woman's Club which maintained it in their Spanish style clubhouse until it outgrew the clubhouse space and moved in 1990 to the former carriage house, donated to the library by James and Richard Oughton. In 1992 the Dwight Public Library became the Prairie Creek Public Library District. The building is listed on the National Register of Historic Places.

Photo courtesy of Anne Martin

Prairie Creek Public Library District

501 Carriage House Lane
Dwight, Illinois 60420

Dedication: 1895 as Oughton Mansion Carriage House

Rededication: 1991 as Dwight Public Library (Renamed Prairie Creek Public Library District in 1992)

Architecture: Carriage House with Classic Influence

Pulaski County Public Library

107 North Main Street
Somerset, Kentucky
42501

Dedication: 1913 as
United States Post
Office

Rededication: 1972 as
Pulaski County Public
Library

Architecture: Italian
Renaissance/Classical
Revival

Photo courtesy of Roger's Studio

Pulaski County Public Library

Somerset, Kentucky

The Pulaski County Public Library building in Somerset, Kentucky continues to be a popular gathering place for Pulaski County citizens. Originally designed as a United States Post Office by architect James Knox Taylor, the structure now encompasses 68,000 volumes and numerous casette and video tapes. In addition, the building is home to the Pulaski County Literacy Council, the Pulaski County Historical Society and a community room available for use by area civic groups.

Taylor's use of masonry and stone exterior cladding closely reflects the original Italian Renaissance prototypes. The formal balance of the massive structure is pronounced by Doric columns supporting a large entablature over the main entrance. The finely toothed design on the entablature continues around the building. Egg and dart detail adorn the area between the necking and the abacus of the column capitals. These details, along with the three parallel vertical channels or triglyphs and the metopes between the channels, all point to the Italian Renaissance style. Contractor R.P. Farnsworth and Company completed the building in 1913 at a cost of nearly $50,000.

With the help of Senator John Sherman Cooper, Attorney Ben Smith and Attorney Don Cooper (the Senator's brother), the Library Board of Trustees received a deed for the former United States Post Office with the stipulation that the building must be used as a library for 25 years before it will become the property of the library board. A $250,000 remodeling in 1972 added a second floor to the interior of the building and converted the structure to library use. The Pulaski County Public Library operates three branch libraries as well as a bookmobile.

Putnam Public Library

327 North Main Street
Nashville, Michigan
49073

Dedication: 1885 as
Putnam residence

Rededication: 1923 as
Putnam Public Library

Architecture: Italianate

Photo courtesy of J-Ad Graphics, Hastings, Michigan

Putnam Public Library

Nashville, Michigan

The Putnam Public Library building in Nashville, Michigan first served as the principal residence of Mr. and Mrs. Charles Putnam. The Italianate structure was constructed during 1884-1885 of bricks manufactured locally by William Boston. While the building cost less than $6,000 to construct, it included elegant Belgian stained glass windows, double brick-wall construction, extensive wood trim, intricate grille-work and an impressive open stairway.

The two-story house features a wrap-around porch with white wooden columns. Tall windows accent the building's height and the low pitched roof, heavy brackets and wide eaves accentuate the trademark Italianate style. White shutters frame the windows while a rounded door offers entrance into the interior.

Putnam died in 1918. His will, executed after his wife's death two years later, deeded the house and property to the Village of Nashville with the stipulation that their home be used for a library named the Putnam Public Library. The will also provided $1,000 for the conversion of the home into a public library. Putnam also designated $10,000 to be used as an endowment to support the library.

The Nashville Women's Literacy Club obtained permission from the Village to establish the library and on September 1, 1923, the library was opened to patrons. A 1989 addition funded completely by local donations houses a children's room, a work room and an office. The Putnam Public Library is listed in the Michigan Registry of Historical Buildings.

St. Charles Public Library District

One South Sixth Avenue
St. Charles, Illinois
60174

Dedication: 1908 as
original Carnegie
Library Building

Rededication: 1964/
1988 as new additions
to St. Charles Public
Library (Renamed St.
Charles Public Library
District in 1978)

Architecture: Classical
Revival/Contemporary

Photo courtesy of JoAnne Laudolff, Library staff member

St. Charles Public Library District
St. Charles, Illinois

The St. Charles Library Association came into being in 1889 as a subscription library with an annual membership fee of $2.00. Its first permanent home at 203 East Main Street (formerly Judge W.D. Barry's law office where a young Abe Lincoln was rumored to have consulted on legal matters) served the community for a number of years.

The library became a public library in 1906 and that same year received a $12,500 grant from the Carnegie Foundation supplemented by local donations totaling $2,500. Chicago architects Phillips, Rogers and Woodyat designed the 7,000-square-foot building which was dedicated in 1908. A 1925 expansion added a mezzanine while a pine-paneled children's room was completed in 1933 under a Civil Works Administration Program.

In 1964 the Geneva, Illinois architectural firm of Frazier, Raftery, Orr and Fairbank designed a new building with 7,640 square feet of ground floor space and 3,950 square feet of basement area. The new structure complemented the brick of the original Carnegie Library. The Children's Department relocated to a remodeled basement in 1973. The renovation was made possible in large part by a donation from the Thomas Rossetter family in memory of their son Bob. A 35,000 square foot addition designed by Wendt Cederholm Tippens, Inc. of Winnetka, Illinois opened in 1988. A donation by Dellora A. and Lester J. Norris funded the 1989 renovation of the 1908 Carnegie building which now houses the library's business, local history and genealogy collections. The original Carnegie pillared entrance has been preserved. Patrons now enter the library through a new ground level entrance. Voters approved conversion of the township library to a library district in 1978. The library applied for inclusion in the National Register of Historic Places in mid-1995.

Tomah Public Library

716 Superior Avenue
Tomah, Wisconsin
54660

Dedication: 1917

Architecture: Prairie

Photo courtesy of John Froelich, Tomah Newspapers

Tomah Public Library
Tomah, Wisconsin

Tomah, Wisconsin derives its name from the French pronunciation of the Menomonee Indian Chief Thomas Carron's first name, "Tomah." The library movement in Tomah originated in 1871 with the establishment of a library in a room of a local Tomah business, The Picture Gallery. The library was maintained through subscription memberships and the donation of books and magazines. Weekly fees were instituted at twenty cents for men and ten cents for women.

Several years later, the Ladies Library Association formed to promote interest in and raise money for the library. In 1875 the subscription library board turned the operation of the library over to the Ladies Library Association and the library was moved to the Main Street home of Sarah Palmer.

In 1881 the growing library moved into a corner of the village's board room, separated by a rope barrier. Five years later, the city assumed full responsibility for operation of the library with an annual appropriation for books and operation. The library officially opened as a free public library on December 31, 1902.

The library acquired the centrally located Whitfield property in 1903 and the library collection moved from the city council room into the house, after modifications were made to the structure.

Former resident, Ernest Buckley, left a $12,000 bequest in 1911 for a library or to purchase land for a city park. The city set aside $7,000 for a library building and used the remainder to buy park land. The approval of a Carnegie Grant in the amount of $10,000 in 1915 provided the remaining money for library construction.

Madison, Wisconsin architects Louis Ward Claude and Edward F. Starck designed a red brick Prairie style structure which was built by A. Kelly of Madison. The four-sided hip roof is covered with green-glazed clay tile. The overhanging roof shelters a foliated design terra cotta frieze. Leaded glass windows and carved stone add other embellishment. The new library was dedicated in 1917. A 1980 addition designed by Potter, Lawson & Pawlowsky of Madison doubled the size of the library. The Tomah Public Library was placed on the National Register of Historic Places in 1976.

Wakefield Public Library
Wakefield, Kansas

The Wakefield Public Library was established in 1914 with a volunteer run library and donated books located in members' homes. In 1930 Wakefield set up a mill levy and established a permanent library room. Although the Wakefield Public Library building resembles a church, its construction in 1937 and dedication on February 5, 1938, was for the original purpose as a library. The WPA (Works Progress Administration) undertook the construction with stone obtained from the nearby farm of Wava Schweitzer. The architect, Mr. Kraybill, received the sum of $114.00 for his design work. One of the stone masons who worked on the library project, Ed Barrett, is alive and lives in Junction City, Kansas.

The original design called for 4,000 volumes to be housed on one floor. In 1970 the basement was cleaned out and the children's section was moved into that space. Currently, the library holds nearly 10,000 volumes.

Fern Normandin served as a librarian from 1928 to her retirement in 1990. Her regular salary in the early years amounted to the grand sum of twenty-five cents a week but she received extra pay for starting her own fires to heat the building.

Reading programs are financed by the Wakefield Library Club, McDonald's Corporation and the American Library Association. As a member of the North Central Kansas Libraries, Wakefield Public Library patrons have wider access to resources.

Photo courtesy of Fred Tillisch

Wakefield Public Library

Third & Dogwood
Wakefield, Kansas
67487

Dedication: 1938

Architecture: American
Vernacular

Wauseon Public Library

117 East Elm Street
Wauseon, Ohio 43567

Dedication: 1906

Rededication: 1986

Architecture: Federal

Photo courtesy of Thomas W. Orth, Copyright © 1994

Wauseon Public Library
Wauseon, Ohio

The Women's Christian Temperance Crusade sponsored Wauseon, Ohio's early library reading room. In 1875 the Citizens Library Association established a subscription library funded by $3 annual membership dues plus a book donation. For more than a quarter of a century, the library travelled from church to private homes to stores, finally relocating to the Courthouse Board of Elections Room.

Seeking more permanent quarters for their library, Wauseon citizens petitioned Andrew Carnegie for a $7,500 library construction grant in 1903. The Federal style building opened on May 26, 1906. Prominent features include the multicolored brickwork, stone corners and Georgian white dormers with intricate panes. The word LIBRARY is inscribed over the main entrance which is flanked by fluted pilasters.

Funded by a Federal grant, the library's own building fund and a bond issue, the 1984-1986 renovation and expansion enhanced the Wauseon Public Library's ability to serve its patrons. The addition, designed by the Cleveland architectural firm of Koster and Associates, blends into the texture of the original library and doubles the available floor space.

Wauseon Public Library is a member of the Northwest Library District and also part of an automated circulation network of several public libraries and two academic libraries.

Webb City Public Library

101 South Liberty
Webb City, Missouri
64870

Dedication: 1915

Architecture:
Richardsonian
Romanesque

Photo courtesy of Bob Foos, Webb City Sentinel

Webb City Public Library
Webb City, Missouri

Webb City's first movement for the establishment of a public library originated in 1910 with the Civic Improvement Association working to develop public sentiment in 1912 for a vote approving tax legislation to support a public library. The tax measure passed in April 1913 and later that month Webb City obtained a $25,000 Carnegie Grant.

Chicago architect Grant C. Miller of Miller, Fullenwider & Dowling used native limestone boulders combined with Carthage stone to design an impressive Richardsonian Romanesque structure reminiscent of a church. This one and a half-story temple of knowledge employs arched windows accented by stained glass panels. Inside, warm red oak interior finish and furniture invite patrons to relax. A unique feature, an interior swinging door is inlaid with stained glass. Arched windows frame each side of the door.

During the early 1930s with the library running low on funds, the Civic Club raised money to keep the library open by selling "red tags" on the city streets. During World War II, the library operated as a Red Cross bandage rolling center.

In 1967 an explosion at the nearby Hercules Powder Plant sent shock waves through the ground, causing damage to the library's floors and walls. Renovations put the library back into shape and also added improved lighting. Webb City Public Library has provided over 80 years of service to city patrons.

Willard Library
Evansville, Indiana

Evansville philanthropist Willard Carpenter endowed the Willard Library in 1876 "for the use of the people of all classes, races and sexes, free of charge, forever." Mr. Carpenter was also instrumental in bringing the Wabash and Erie Canal to Evansville.

The library was originally planned by architects Boyd and Brickley. However, the financial depression of the late 1870s forced the abandonment of planning and construction for five years. Later, architects James and Merritt Reid took over with an Italianate/Venetian Gothic Style. The Willard Library was finally completed in 1884 and opened in 1885. It now holds the distinction as the oldest public library building in Indiana and is listed on the National Register of Historic Places.

The building is constructed of red brick with limestone used for effective contrast. Architecturally interesting features include a stately corner stair tower encompassing the entrance, mansard roof with heavy dormer windows, cornice turrets and window arcades supported by modified Byzantine columns. The library is surrounded by a four-and-a-half acre park dedicated for public use.

Inside: ornately carved woodwork, massive brass hardware (dated 1883), fireplaces, and multicolored tile carry through the architectural theme. Three colored glass rondels in second story gable end windows depict Homer, Shakespeare and Mr. Carpenter. The Willard Library possesses an extensive collection of primary sources on the history of Southern Indiana.

Photo courtesy of Jerome, Special Collections, Willard Library

Willard Library

21 First Avenue
Evansville, Indiana 47710

Dedication: 1885

Architecture: Italianate/Venetian Gothic

IV. Rocky Mountain and Western Region

Campbell County Public Library

2101 4-J Road
Gillette, Wyoming
82718

Dedication: 1983

Architecture:
Contemporary

Photo courtesy of James A. Frost, The News-Record

Recluse Branch Campbell County Public Library

Recluse Community
Hall
Recluse, Wyoming
82725

Dedication: 1934

Architecture:
American Rustic

Photo courtesy of Campbell County Public Library

Campbell County Public Library

Gillette, Wyoming

The first community library, operated by a local woman's club, began in a small attic room of the Campbell County Courthouse in May 1928. A year later, the County Commissioners created the Campbell County Public Library and established a Board of Trustees. The fledgling library operated out of a small building once used by the Courthouse custodian.

In 1941 area rancher George Amos donated $21,000 for the construction of the George Amos Memorial Library, now a branch library. The current 32,000-square-foot library on 4-J Road was dedicated in 1983 and features a central atrium with clerestory windows. The George Amos Room, constructed of glass and moss rock, houses Amos's rare book collection and the library's fine art collection. Gillette architect Christopher Hard integrated local materials into the contemporary design.

Outside, the Sheepherders' Monument reflects the area's history. The stonework was moved from a ranch southeast of Gillette. Sheepherders built the stone "johnnies" of flat native stone to mark a special summit. Created by Wheatland, Wyoming sculptor, Carl Jensen, the rider represents rancher George Amos. Neither the rider nor the sheepherder wear guns, signifying the peace that existed between the ranchers and sheepherders in Campbell County.

Recluse Branch Library
Recluse, Wyoming

The Recluse Branch Library first organized in 1927 as The Pleasant Hour Club. The library eventually moved into the Recluse Community Hall, built in 1934 from logs cut and hauled by local residents. The library's books are located in a wall cupboard that is opened to allow patrons to peruse the collection.

Carnegie Public Library

Las Vegas, New Mexico

Built to last, the Las Vegas, New Mexico Carnegie Public Library remains the only Carnegie Library in the state still in use as a library. The Las Vegas library movement originated in 1887 when the Women's Christian Temperance Union emphasized the benefits of a reading room in reaching "young men who would use the room and be out of the reach of temptation." The reading room opened in 1893 as one of the first in the Territory of New Mexico.

On March 26, 1902, the Las Vegas City Council adopted a resolution pledging $1,000 in annual maintenance funds if the Carnegie Foundation would grant $10,000 toward the construction of a library. Controversy arose over the chosen site location in a hillsite park because it was not centrally located. A court opinion settled the matter, allowing the council to proceed building on the hillsite location.

Construction began in 1903 on a domed building in the form of a Greek cross designed by the architect, Mr. Martin. The contractor, J.E. Consaul, used red brick accented by white stones and white wooden dental detailing and large columns flanking the entrance. Other features include arched window heads and modillion cornices with red brick coping opening to a white balustrade above the entrance porch. The Carnegie Public Library achieved New Mexico State Register of Cultural Properties status in 1974 and was placed on the National Register of Historic Places in 1978.

Photo courtesy of Jean Streetman, The Las Vegas Optic

Carnegie Public Library

500 National Avenue
Las Vegas, New Mexico
87701

Dedication: 1904

Architecture: Palladian

Chapman Branch Library

Salt Lake City, Utah

Considered one of the finest Carnegie Libraries in the West, the Chapman Branch Library of the Salt Lake City Public Library System almost lost Carnegie sponsorship at the very onset. A reference to this shaky beginning was made at the 1938 memorial service for Joseph Don Carlos (Carl) Young, the Chapman Branch Library architect. John D. Spencer, chairman of the Salt Lake City Public Library Board of Directors, gave the following remarks.

Carnegie's representative, James Bertram took a large blue pencil and slashed it through Young's plans, exclaiming, "This is a great waste of space."

Young jumped to his feet, seized the blueprints and said, "I don't know and I don't care who or what you are, or how many millions you control, you can't insult me like this and get away with it." Folding his plans, he left the room, slamming the door behind him.

I said, "Mr. Bertram, you have made a wrong estimate of Mr. Young and I approve of his resent-ment and anger.... You have no finer architects in New York than he and no finer buildings than those of his making.... If this library is to be built it must be built without a single change of any kind."

Bertram reconsidered and Carnegie approved the grant for the full $25,000 requested. Incidentally, that was the only Carnegie Grant for library construction in Salt Lake City. Young designed a magnificent brick structure with four imposing Tuscan columns guarding the rounded arch portal.

Record-breaking snowfall in 1992 collapsed the roof of the Chapman Branch Library. Fortunately, ninety-five percent of the library's collection remained undamaged. The building has been completely restored and refurbished to serve future generations. The Chapman Branch Library is listed on the Utah and National Register of Historic Places.

Photo courtesy of Salt Lake City Public Library

Chapman Branch Library

The Salt Lake City
Public Library System

577 South 900 West
Salt Lake City, Utah
84104

Dedication: 1917

Architecture: Classical
Revival

Chouteau County Free Library

1518 Main Street
Fort Benton, Montana
59442

Dedication: 1918

Architecture: Prairie

Photo courtesy of Tim Burmeister, River Press

Chouteau County Free Library

Fort Benton, Montana

Eight women from the Study Club (later renamed the Fort Benton Woman's Club) were literally the driving force behind the Chouteau County Free Library. In borrowed cars, they drove rutted and muddy roads across the county in order to obtain signatures for their petition to create a free library.

Chouteau earned the distinction of being among the first Montana counties to formally establish a county library in 1915. The next year, the women had opened a reading room for children and library services for adults.

Mrs. Dorothy McLeish, the leader of the Study Club, proclaimed, "There is no city so great that it does not wear its library as its chief jewel."

In 1916 a $15,000 Carnegie Grant provided the funds to construct a new library building. Fort Benton resident Joseph Hirshberg donated the building site in memory of his wife and the Commercial Club provided two adjoining lots.

Architect George Carsley used brick and Prairie architecture to achieve the clean, forthright lines of the library. The original Carnegie Library (now called the Chouteau County Free Library) opened its doors in October 1918. A 1994 addition, funded by an anonymous bequest, doubled the library's capacity but remained true to the building's original architecture with the same style windows, brick configuration and warm wood molding.

Cochise County Library District
Bisbee, Arizona

The Cochise County Library District is housed in the Old High School Building, Bisbee's first high school constructed in 1914 at a cost of $80,000. The building was designed for the historic mining town by Los Angeles architect Norman F. March.

A unique feature of the building derives from Bisbee's hilly terrain. The basement and three above ground floors of the building all open onto a street level. This configuration allows for moving books and records between floors with ease. Library employees move them from floor to floor by way of the street level entrances without having to maneuver up flights of stairs.

A fire ravaged the building on December 16, 1919, with the total destruction of the science laboratory and domestic science room and damage to most of the build-ing, but the outer walls were left intact for the most part. Students attended other schools in the community while the high school was rebuilt in 1920. In 1958 Bisbee built a new high school and the old school was purchased by Cochise County for use as the Cochise County Library District and other county office space.

The Italian Renaissance structure features a rounded portico and dental molding accenting the building's size. Other Italian Renaissance elements include the rusticated masonry near the entrance and the important cornice. The library is located on the second floor. The Cochise County Library District facility represents an excellent example of a fine building with historical significance being rescued for other community uses.

Photo courtesy of Bisbee Mining and Historical Museum

Cochise County Library District

Second Floor
Old High School
Building
Drawer AK
Bisbee, Arizona 85603

Dedication: 1914 as
Bisbee High School

Rededication: 1958 as
Cochise County Library
District (second floor)

Architecture: Italian
Renaissance

Cooper Landing Library
Cooper Landing, Alaska

True to the Alaskan tradition of independence and of making do with what is available at hand, the Cooper Landing Library south of Anchorage on the Kenai Peninsula was crafted of native Alaskan logs by premier log cabin architect, Tom Walker.

The library, in this community of some 400 people, is situated in the picturesque Cooper Landing Community Park near the Kenai River. Nearby, salmon runs and bald eagles keep nature close at hand. Cooper Landing residents take ownership in their library seriously as evidenced by the staff which is composed entirely of volunteers.

While libraries in the "outside" took pride in converting their libraries' heat sources from coal or fireplace methods of the turn of the century to more modern conveniences such as gas and oil furnaces, Copper Landing library patrons revel in the cozy warmth of the heat thrown off from the wood burning stove. The supplemental electrical heat is used only when absolutely necessary.

Contributions from residents and a state grant provided the construction monies. The traditional looking log building features a number of add-ons, such as a large porch overhang and a wheelchair ramp and decking for the convenience of library patrons. Walker, also a noted photographer, had a hand in furnishing the library with a selection of his photographs. It is an inviting place to find a cozy chair and read a good book while listening to the crackling fire.

Photo courtesy of David Rhode

Cooper Landing Library

Community Park-
Bean Creek Road
Cooper Landing, Alaska
99572

Dedication: 1984

Architecture: American
Rustic

Coronado Public Library

Coronado, California

The Coronado Public Library originated in 1890 with the establishment of the Coronado Library and Free Reading Room Association. In 1895 the Hotel del Coronado leased its Spring House pavilion to the fledgling library for $50 per year, with the first two years rental given as a donation. Around 1900 John D. Spreckels, West Coast sugar and shipping magnate, bought out the hotel and gifted the Spring House to the city. In 1909 Spreckels donated the land and funds to construct a new library building.

Architect Harrison Albright of San Diego designed the Coronado Public Library in the Classical Revival style. The 1700 square foot library cost $10,000. Additions to the building took place in 1935, 1957 and 1961 and added another 6000 square feet of library space. In 1974 another San Diego architect, Homer Delawie, designed the library expansion while retaining the earlier ornate entrance to the new structure. The original white concrete columns and tall doors and windows deliver a sense of classic elegance, linking Coronado's past and future.

Near the entrance, the Harlow Memorial Rose Garden welcomes visitors to the library. Delawie's use of glass walls invites the outdoors in with plenty of natural light.

Displays of Coronado's historical treasures, the work of local artists and the interior garden courtyards add to the reputation of the Coronado Public Library as a true community resource and cultural center.

Photo courtesy of Christian Esquevin

Coronado Public Library

640 Orange Avenue
Coronado, California 92118

Dedication: 1909

Architecture: Classical Revival

Elbert County Library

Kiowa, Colorado

Originally constructed in 1903 as St. Ann Catholic Church, the structure now housing the Elbert County Library still draws people religiously in this community of several hundred located Southeast of Denver.

The one-story American Vernacular structure was crafted from hand-cut stone quarried south of Kiowa in the Hangman's Point area and hauled to the site by mule team. Local labor and volunteer parishioners erected the church. A steep gabled roof frames the front door and windows, arched in Romanesque style. Over the main entrance, a round stained glass window with an anchor pattern and a granite cross give testimony to the building's original purpose. Inside, a cathedral ceiling provides a fitting setting for the lofty endeavors of reading and learning.

St. Ann's served the community until the 1960s. when the Archdiocese of Denver dissolved many country parishes. Archbishop Casey decided that the closed church should be used for a needed community project. As a result, to solve the problem of limited library space, St. Ann's was rededicated in 1970 as the Elbert County Library and remains in frequent use today.

Photo courtesy of C.J. Prince

Elbert County Library

331 Comanche Street,
Kiowa, Colorado 80117

Dedication: 1903 as St. Ann
Catholic Church

Rededication: 1970 as Elbert
County Library

Architecture: American
Vernacular

Everett Public Library

Everett, Washington

The Everett Public Library began as a volunteer effort by the local women's club and was originally housed in a room at the Everett City Hall. This group of women built a collection for the library by soliciting gift books from women's clubs around the country. In 1903 Everett received a $25,000 Carnegie grant and built a fine Italianate structure which served the city well over the next quarter century before library usage outgrew the available space. Through special permission of the Carnegie Foundation, the city sold the building and it operated as a funeral parlor for years. It is now owned by the county government and listed on the National Register of Historic Places.

The current library building opened to the public on October 3, 1934, and represents a superb example of the Art Moderne style of architecture to symbolize Everett's growth as an industrial city. A local industrialist, Leonard Howarth, donated $75,000 for the new library construction. Pacific Northwest architect Carl F. Gould enhanced his design with interior art work of regional artists such as painter Guy Anderson, muralist J.T. Jacobsen, and sculptor Dudley Pratt plus paintings purchased through the Public Works Art Program.

The 1991 award-winning expansion and renovation project by Cardwell/Thomas & Associates, assisted by Dykeman Architects, represents an excellent example of how a community can retain the original unique architecture and design while continuing to meet the community's growing needs with a doubling of capacity and the addition of new services. Highlights of the expansion include a two-story rotunda and a barrel-vaulted main reading room. Following Gould's lead, the inclusion of the work of several noteworthy artists compliments the expansion.

An early innovator due to space restrictions, the library broke new ground with initiation of the first Washington State library bookmobile to reach its patrons.

Photo courtesy of Cardwell/Thomas & Associates, Seattle, Washington

Everett Public Library

2702 Hoyt Avenue
Everett, Washington
98201

Dedication: 1934

Architecture: Art Moderne

Glendale Public Library

Glendale, Arizona

Ground breaking took place in April 1986 and the Glendale Public Library was dedicated on July 27, 1987. Bond funding for the new library included $5.4 million for construction, $1 million for books and $3 million for furnishings and equipment. The building is beautifully situated within the city-owned Sahuaro Ranch Park, an 80-acre historical site with original ranch buildings, sports facilities, citrus and palm groves and over 100 peacocks.

Phoenix architect J. Barry Moffitt & Associates, Ltd. designed the two-story, 64,000 square foot, sandblasted desert blend colored block structure. It features a skylit central atrium and acid-washed copper covered panels, with obvious ties to Arizona's copper legacy and open skies. Inside, the Glendale Arts Commission exhibits a number of fine art pieces including a 5' by 30' mural by space artist, Robert McCall; an 8' by 18' painting depicting Glendale's heritage by Howard Post and a piece of art by noted Indian sculptor, Allan Houser. Outside, a life-sized bronze, "The Irrigators," by Debbie Gessner and a nearby reflecting pool grace the entrance. The library's xeriscape garden garnered a 1994 Environmental Excellence Award from the Valley Forward Association.

Glendale has come a long way since the Glendale Public Library Association sold shares for $5 each in 1898. One of the original certificates is on display by the library.

Photo courtesy of Paul Zampini

Glendale Public Library

5959 West Brown Street
Glendale, Arizona
85302

Dedication: 1987

Architecture:
Contemporary

Hawaii State Library

478 South King Street
Honolulu, Hawaii 96813

Dedication: 1913

Architecture:
Renaissance Revival

Photo courtesy of Paul H. Mark, Hawaii State Public Library System

Hawaii State Library

Honolulu, Hawaii

The Hawaii Territorial Legislature passed an Act in 1907, formally establishing the Library of Hawaii. After several years of contact with Andrew Carnegie, he finally approved $100,000 in December 1909 for the construction of the Library of Hawaii. In addition, the Legislature approved another $27,000 toward the building and grounds.

New York architect and brother of Mrs. Carnegie, Henry D. Whitfield, in association with Henry L. Kerr of Honolulu, designed the two-storied library in the Renaissance Revival style. Large white columns and rounded window arches give the appearance of majesty. Situated in Honolulu near the Hawaii State Capital and Iolani Palace, the library's green tiled roof blends into the surrounding garden-like setting of palms and other native plants. An open-air courtyard with tropical plants remains a favorite library patron haven.

The 20,300-square-foot structure originally had capacity for 100,000 volumes but proved inadequate by 1925 when the Hawaii Legislature approved land acquisition funding for future expansion. Additions in 1929 and 1992 included the Children's Room; a new Reading Room; a Business, Science & Technology wing; a third floor for office space and nearly 80,000 square feet for the library's more than 500,000 volumes.

A mural depicting various Hawaiian legends completed by Juliet May Fraser in 1935 graces the Edna Allyn Room (formerly the Children's Room). The Hawaii and Pacific Room was renamed after Samuel Manaiakalani Kamakau, a noted Hawaiian historian. The Hawaii State Library is listed on the National Register of Historic Places and included in the Hawaii Capital Historic District.

Hearst Free Library

Anaconda, Montana

The Hearst Free Library in Anaconda, Montana owes its existence to Mrs. Phoebe Hearst, wife of Senator George Hearst. Hearst made his fortune in gold mining in Utah and copper mining in Montana. Mr. Hearst died in 1892 and his wife had sold her interest in the copper mining company by 1895 but she never lost her affection for Anaconda.

In 1895 she opened a reading room at 308 Cherry Street. The overwhelming reception of the reading room by Anaconda citizens inspired her to build the Hearst Free Library as a memorial to her husband. In addition to providing the funds for construction of the library, Mrs. Hearst maintained the building at her own expense from 1898 to 1903 when she presented the library to the City of Anaconda as a Christmas gift. She also donated $1,000 a year for three years for the purpose of acquiring books.

Noted San Francisco architect Frank S. Van Trees achieved a sense of power and majesty using Roman Revival lines embellished by two stalwart granite columns with Corinthian capitals. The great spreading half circle arches of the windows and the pilasters carry this theme throughout the balance of the facade and other sides of the building.

Granite steps lead up to a deep landing as patrons enter the library through a large rounded portico. Likewise, the first story windows are rounded while the upper story windows are rectangular. Fittingly in copper country, the trussed roof and copper cornice rest upon the entablature frieze. Inside a marble bust of Senator Hearst greets visitors. In 1973 The Hearst Free Library earned a place on the National Register of Historic Places.

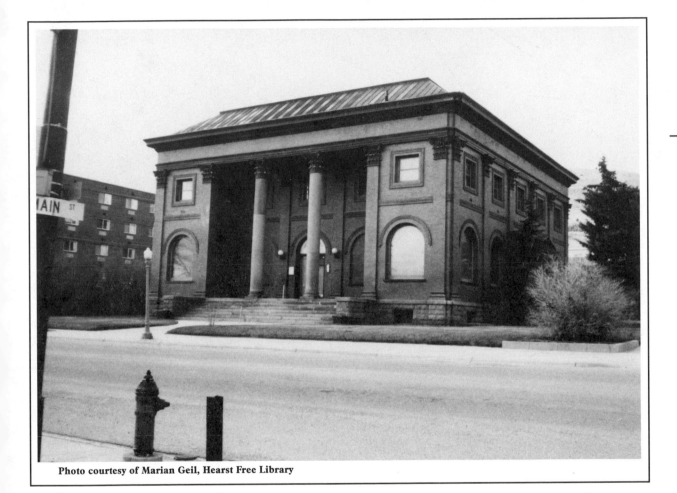

Photo courtesy of Marian Geil, Hearst Free Library

Hearst Free Library

401 Main Street
Anaconda, Montana
59711

Dedication: 1898

Architecture: Roman
Revival

Lordsburg-Hidalgo Library

208 East Third Street
Lordsburg, New Mexico
88045

Dedication: 1937

Architecture: Pueblo

Photo courtesy of Brenda Collins, Lordsburg Liberal

Lordsburg-Hidalgo Library
Lordsburg, New Mexico

The Lordsburg Women's Club initiated the drive for a library by going from house to house asking for donations of books in 1919. The first library operated out of the lobby of the Star Theater in 1920 and moved several times in the next few years to two small houses and the Egon News Stand. From 1927 to 1935 the Lordsburg-Hidalgo Library occupied part of the basement of the Hidalgo County Court House, in spaces as small as 9 x 15 feet. Beginning in 1932, the library discontinued the membership fee with the enactment of taxes to maintain the library.

A combination of Lordsburg city budget, Hidalgo County budget and the Library's sinking fund provided the money to construct a library building, completed in July 1937. The Pueblo style architecture and adobe construction particularly suit the town's location in southwestern New Mexico. Likewise, the interior maintains a southwest theme.

Originally, the building also housed the Health Department and Justice of the Peace. People often stop in at the Lordsburg-Hidalgo Library to revisit the place where they were married. Today, the library occupies the entire building with the addition of a Reference Room, Southwestern Room and Spanish Room. In the Children's Room, stained glass windows commemorate the memory of early pioneer families. It is one of only two county libraries in the State of New Mexico.

Multnomah County Library

205 Northeast Russell
Street
Portland, Oregon 97212

Dedication: 1913

Architecture: Georgian

Photo courtesy of Multnomah County Library

Multnomah County Library
Portland, Oregon

Multnomah County Library in Portland, Oregon exhibits a wealth of art and literary history through its architecture and detailing. Architect Albert E. Doyle combined a base and first floor of Bedford limestone with upper floors of red brick for a pleasing appearance. Limestone trimming and balustrades frame the brick and bring unity to the building. The Georgian structure features rounded windows and entrances.

Friezes, carvings and inscriptions represent historic printers, novelists, historians, inventors, philosophers, poets and dramatists and scientists as well as subjects such as Architecture, Chemistry, Education, Engineering, Literature, Mathematics, Philosophy, Poetry, Religion and Travel. There are seventy-five pedestals in the balustrade and the larger ones are carved with the Seal of the United States, the Early Oregon Territorial Seal, the State Seal, the County Seal and the Seal of the Library Association of Portland.

Carved above the center door of the main entrance, Alpha and Omega reside in an open book. Inside, public halls and stairways consist of pink Tennessee marble with accents of fumed oak. Art work on display throughout the library ranges from a 1930 sculpture of "Alice in Wonderland" (a WPA project by artist Florence Thomas) to an oil painting, inspired by petrographs and petroglyphs, by Portland artist Byron Gardner to an 1890 bronze "Pan of Rohallion," sculpted in Paris by world renowned Frederick William MacMonnies.

The Multnomah County Library was dedicated in 1913 and placed on the National Register of Historic Places in 1979. A major renovation effort is targeted for completion in 1997.

Nevada State Library and Archives

Carson City, Nevada

The $20 million Nevada State Library and Archives "wraps around" the original State Printing Office, constructed in 1866 and later home to the State of Nevada Archives. The building's design incorporates touches of the stonework present in the historic archives building as well as the nearby state capitol. The new structure's roof line with several prominent peaks repeats throughout an elaborate foyer and replicates the Carson City skyline of the nearby Washoe Mountain Range and echoes the historic roof.

Designed by Las Vegas architects Edward DeLorenzo and Mark Stika, the 130,000-square-foot Nevada State Library and Archives encompasses capacity for more than 95,000 volumes and 700,000 federal and state publications. The glass-walled lobby covered with the dynamic roofline mentioned above provides easy access to collections and services housed behind the buff-colored brick portions of the facility. Windows in the Research Room offer dramatic views of the State Capitol.

Outside, a landscaped courtyard borders the craggy brown limestone exterior of the historic building which previously stored the Nevada State Archives. An exhibits gallery possesses an expansive view of the trees and statuary on the capitol grounds.

For those wishing to view the imposing brick Victorian old Nevada Federal Building (circa 1891), the State Library location from 1972-1992, a several block walk to 401 North Carson Street transports you back to another century.

Nevada State Library and Archives

100 Stewart Street
Carson City, Nevada 89710

Dedication: 1992

Architecture: Contemporary

Niobrara County Library

Lusk, Wyoming

Niobrara County Library in Lusk, Wyoming ranks as the last remaining Carnegie Library in Wyoming still operating in the original Carnegie Library building. It has been proposed for listing on the National Register of Historic Places. In essence, except for minor changes such as carpeting and a new furnace, the Niobrara County Library remains the same as the day it was built.

The first library in Niobrara County, Stillman Public Library, occupied part of the old Masonic Building in 1913. It was named in honor of Lusk's only centenarian, Mrs. Sarah M. Stillman, grandmother of Frank S. Lusk, co-founder of Lusk. The Stillman Library moved several times before the house in which it was located was badly damaged in a January 1919 fire.

Earlier, the Civic Improvement Club (formerly the Lusk Reading Club) approached Mr. Andrew Carnegie for funds to construct a library. Carnegie responded with a grant for $11,000 on May 8, 1914. The Finance Committee of the Civic Improvement Club conducted a subscription drive which collected $550 to purchase lots for the library's building site in 1917. However, the Niobrara County Board of Commissioners did not approve a resolution accepting the Carnegie Grant and agreeing to the maintenance conditions until July 3, 1918.

Local contractor Elmer H. Ranck completed the building in 1919 and the library has served the community well for over seventy-five years. The structure features an arched transom over the main entrance, a theme that is carried to the rest of the building with arched windows. The words, Carnegie Library, are inscribed over the main entrance.

Photo courtesy of Jim Headley, Lusk Herald

Niobrara County Library

425 South Main Street
Lusk, Wyoming 82225

Dedication: 1919

Architecture:
Renaissance/Italianate

Queen Anne Branch Library

Seattle Public Library
400 West Garfield
Street
Seattle, Washington
98119

Dedication: 1914

Architecture: English
Gothic

Photo courtesy of Seattle Public Library, Greg Farrar

Queen Anne Branch Library
Seattle, Washington

Ever since the Women's Christian Temperance Union opened a reading room in North Seattle in the 1890s, area residents worked for a library on Queen Anne Hill. Land for the library was purchased in 1912 with a $500 donation by Queen Anne resident and owner of "The Seattle Times," Colonel Alden J. Blethen, plus $6,700 added by the city. The library dream came to fruition with a $35,000 Carnegie Grant for the construction of the Queen Anne Branch Library, opened in 1914.

The English Gothic style contains classical design elements such as pediments, columns and cornices which blend in with the surrounding neighborhood. Seattle architects Woodruff Marbury Somervell and Harlan Thomas designed the one-story, slate covered hip roofed, brick structure with masonry parapets and terra cotta window surrounds. A skylight provides natural light over the rear stack area. Golden oak panels provide a rich, warm tone to the reading rooms and library interior.

Art-glass windows created by Richard Spaulding, replaced the north windows in 1978, representing one of the largest stained-glass commissions in Seattle. The Seattle architectural firm of Cardwell/Thomas & Associates presided over the 1989 $440,000 renovation, for which the firm was awarded a National Honor Award for sensitive restoration design from the National Trust for Historic Preservation. The Queen Anne Branch Library achieved listing on the National Register of Historic Places in 1982 and was given the Honor Award from the Washington Trust for Historic Preservation and a Citation from the Seattle Landmark Board.

Renton Public Library

100 Mill Avenue South
Renton, Washington
98055

Dedication: 1966

Rededication: 1987

Architecture:
Contemporary

Photo courtesy of Linda Petersen

Renton Public Library

Renton, Washington

Ignazio and Jennie Sartori donated the land for the original 1914 red brick Renton Public Library funded by a $10,000 Carnegie Grant. The land is now part of the beautiful park adjacent to the current library. The Carnegie Library served the community until 1966 when the present library building, funded by the City of Renton through a bond issue approved by the voters, opened to the public. The growth of Renton from a coal mining community of 4,000 to an aerospace community of 32,000 challenged the citizens to support their commitment to the Renton Public Library.

The library adjoins the city's Liberty Park, which comes complete with a hiking and jogging trail that leads to Lake Washington two miles away. The Renton Public Library is probably the only library that spans a river. Library patrons can sit above the eighty-foot wide Cedar River in the fall and observe the largest sockeye salmon run in Washington State.

Designed by the architectural firm of Johnston-Campanella-Murakami & Company, the single-level contemporary brick, glass and stucco structure rests upon a river-spanning bridge situated south of Seattle. Cast red bronze art screens by artist Marvin Herard were presented to the library by Allied Arts of Renton in 1966. An extensive renovation and addition designed by Elaine Day Latourelle & Associates was completed in 1987.

The library houses the Renton Historical Collection and the Washington State Collection which is located in the Sartori Room, named to commemorate the generous contribution by the Sartoris.

Visitors would be hard-pressed to find a more peaceful setting for a library. The Renton Public Library is a haven for books, people and education.

Santa Ana Public Library

26 Civic Center Plaza
Santa Ana, California
92702

Dedication: 1960

Architecture:
Contemporary

Photo courtesy of Santa Ana Public Library

Santa Ana Public Library

Santa Ana, California

The library movement in Santa Ana, California dates back to 1878 with the establishment of the Santa Ana Library Association circulating library for subscribing members. This also coincided with the arrival of the Southern Pacific Railroad in Santa Ana and the subsequent rapid growth of the community. In 1887 the Association merged its library with the Women's Christian Temperance Union reading room, making the book collection available to the general public. The City of Santa Ana took over the W.C.T.U. library in 1891 and levied taxes for its support.

Carnegie granted Santa Ana $15,000 in 1902 for the construction of a new library at Fifth & Sycamore on a lot donated by W. H. Spurgeon, founder of Santa Ana. The Carnegie Library opened in 1903 and served its Santa Ana patrons until 1960 when it was demolished upon the advent of the new Santa Anna Public Library at Civic Center Drive and Ross Street, constructed at a cost of $805,000.

Designed by architect Harold Gimeno of Santa Ana and library consultant Francis Keally of New York, the modern building features curtain walls of glass for efficient natural lighting, smooth uniform texture for a balanced composition, and a flat roof. The tilt-up concrete construction employs Italian Marble facing. Simplicity and efficiency are exemplified by the relative lack of ornamentation. Two medallions, one of Homer and the other of Longfellow, adorn the facade with dignity. The library celebrated its centennial with a $1.28 million renovation in 1991.

A.K. Smiley Public Library

125 West Vine Street
Redlands, California
92373

Dedication: 1898

Architecture:
Romanesque/Mission

Photo courtesy of A.K. Smiley Public Library Archives

A.K. Smiley Public Library

Redlands, California

Early public reading rooms in Redlands gave way to the city's first public library in 1894, located in the Y.M.C.A. building. Soon the need for a larger library became evident and Board of Trustees president Alfred H. Smiley discussed library plans with his twin brother and close associate in upper New York State hotel enterprises, Albert K. Smiley. By March 1897 Albert donated sixteen downtown acres to the city for a park (Smiley Park) and also committed to fund the construction of the A.K. Smiley Public Library. Combined, the park and library cost $60,000 when completed in 1898.

A.K. Smiley also donated the $12,000 required for the 1906 expansion wing while a younger brother, Daniel, gifted $10,000 for the 1920 Children's Room wing. Other additions include the 1926 and 1930 wings donated by E.M. Lyon together with public contributions and a major 1990 expansion funded by city bonds.

Redlands architect T.R. Griffith designed the building in a Romanesque/Mission style and the Redlands contracting firm of Davis M. Donald constructed the brick structure adorned with hand-cut stone trimmings and a red tiled roof. Stained glass windows illustrated themes of learning. The 1926 and 1930 wings were designed by Pasadena architect Myron Hunt. Cathleen Malmstrom and Bruce Judd of the San Francisco Architectural Resources Group served as architects for the 1990 $4.1 million expansion. The general contractor was Donald, McKee and Hart (the firm also built the original 1898 library) of Redlands. The unique architectural quality of the original building was painstakingly preserved. The library is listed on the National Register of Historic Places and as a California State Landmark.

Tacoma Public Library

Tacoma, Washington

In 1901 Tacoma garnered a $75,000 Carnegie Grant for the construction of the Tacoma Public Library, a far cry from the modest beginnings of the subscription circulating library established in 1886 in the home of Mrs. Grace R. Moore.

New members travelled from distant farm lands or small homesteads to obtain the books longed for in their isolated lives. In her 1934 "History of the Tacoma Public Library," Grace Moore described one such early member: "Years spent on a timber claim had made her look as weather-beaten as a pine, but under the rough exterior still flowed the sap of New England Culture. These were the types of settlers it was a pleasure and a privilege to serve."

The Carnegie Library building served the growing community well until the mid-forties when the Tacoma City Council decided to build a new main library adjacent to the existing facility. An earthquake in 1949 caused severe damage to the Carnegie Library, requiring removal of the ornate dome and other architectural details. In 1952 a dull and uninteresting (as described in a 1976 facilities study) 64,700-square-foot structure was attached to the Carnegie Library. It reflected modern architecture and materials with permastone, stainless steel and glass dominating.

Ironically, in later years, space requirements pressed the Carnegie portion back into library use for housing operating collections. Its roof was replaced in 1976 with a Community Development Block Act Grant. The 1952 library was completely remodeled with an award-winning redesign by the Tsang Partnership in 1990. The restoration picked up the horizontal lines and archway architectural details of the Carnegie library to make a unified whole. In addition, the Carnegie Library's columns, rotunda and skylight have also been painstakingly restored.

Photo courtesy of The Tacoma Public Library

Tacoma Public Library

1102 Tacoma Avenue
South
Tacoma, Washington
98402

Dedication: 1903

Rededication: 1952

Rededication: 1990

Architecture: 1903
Italian Renaissance
1952/1990
Contemporary/Art
Moderne

John Tomay Memorial Library
Georgetown, Colorado

The Georgetown Library Association was formed in 1885 and the trustees established the first local reading room in November 1887 in the Barnes Building. As reported in "The Georgetown Courier," "...a place where each will feel that not only a warm, cozy nook and an interesting book but a cordial welcome, also, awaits him." The John Tomay Memorial Library staff works hard to maintain that comfortable atmosphere.

The library is named after John Tomay, a local insurance man who also served as a volunteer fireman, school board member and County Commissioner. Tomay left his entire estate to the Georgetown Library Association. The centrally located land was donated by families who owned several vacant buildings on the proposed site.

Denver architect John J. Huddart utilized the cottage style architecture to create a homelike atmosphere for library patrons. The brick building was constructed by D.G. Wood for $8,600 with the Masonic Lodge of Georgetown overseeing the laying of the cornerstone in 1924. In 1988 John Tomay once again played a role in the expansion of the library. Interest on funds still remaining from the sale of some of Tomay's property provided the $8,000 required to renovate the basement for use as the adult nonfiction collection area. In addition, 600 volunteer hours helped complete the project.

The 2000-square-foot M. Paton Ryan Children's Wing was added in 1992 with over $150,000 derived from grants and fund raising. Designed by Long-Hoeft Architects, the contemporary brick addition blends with the original architecture.

Photo courtesy of Ann Martin

John Tomay Memorial Library

605 Sixth Street
Georgetown, Colorado
80444

Dedication: 1925

Architecture: Cottage

Index